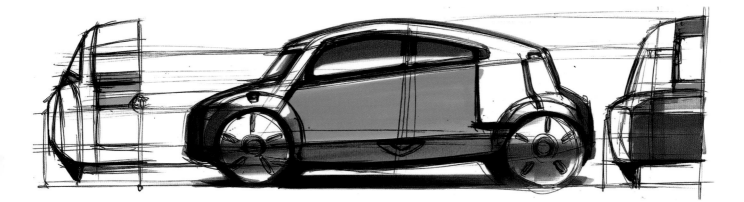

CONCEPT
CARS

METRO BOOKS
New York

text JON STROUD

edited by
VALERIA MANFERTO DE FABIANIS

editorial coordination
LAURA ACCOMAZZO - GIORGIA RAINERI

graphic design
MARINELLA DEBERNARDI

Con/tents

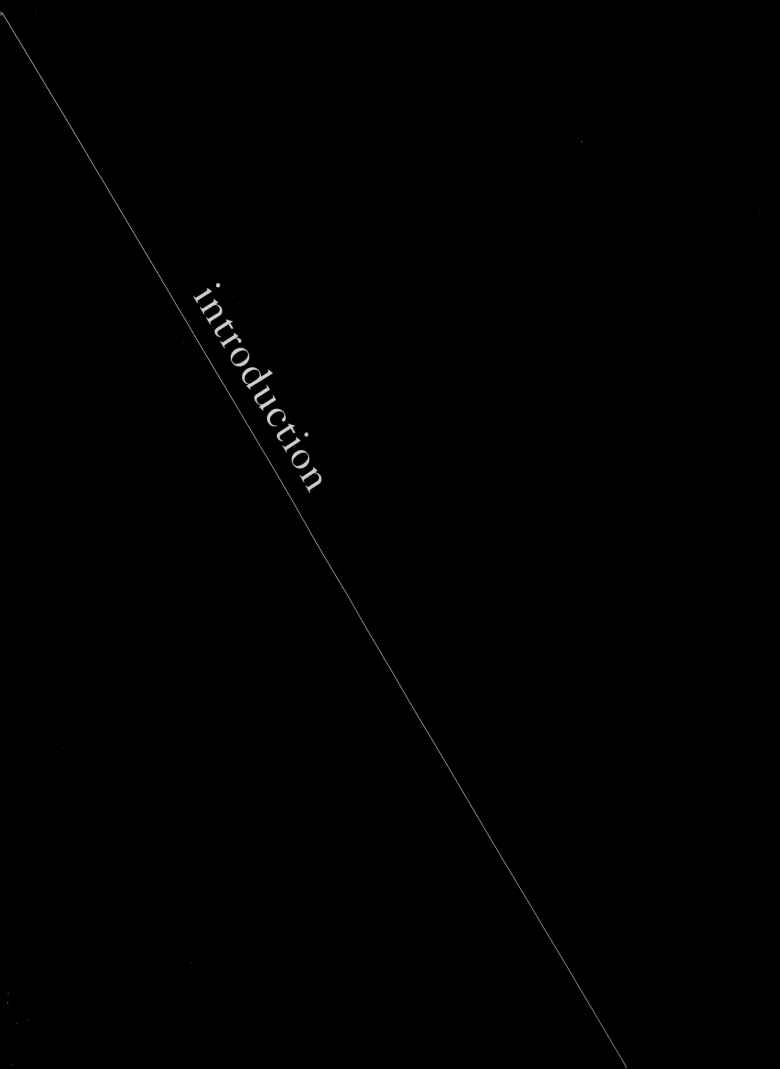

introduction

It was the famous English writer and historian H.G. Wells who brought us the phrase The Shape of Things to Come in the title of his 1933 novel. Wells, like his French contemporary Jules Verne, had an uncanny ability to predict the technologies of the future and between them they foresaw many of the inventions we now take for granted and regularly use on a day-by-day basis. Predicting the future is a far from easy thing to do; trends change, people change, priorities change.

The Californian-born Harley J. Earl, who was appointed director of General Motors' rather curiously named Art & Color Section in 1927, knew the problems of prediction all too well. Already it was clear that engineering and production technologies were moving forward at an astonishing pace; to predict the car of the future would surely be a futile endeavor. Always the showman, Earl's approach was to prove altogether different. Rather than trying to see into the future he decided he would try to influence it – and this he did with the creation, in 1938, of the Buick Y-Job – the world's first true concept car.

Up until this time, cars had taken on an undeniable boxy appearance as if the only tools on hand to their designers had been a drawing board, a pencil and a ruler. There were, of course, some spectacularly beautiful designs but the overrul-

ing design philosophy of the age and of the
prevalent production methods all followed an
identical track – a squared-off bonnet was com-
plemented by a radiator grille of architectural pro-
portions, open wheels were covered only by flimsy
cycle-style fenders joined by hefty side-mounted running boards, both front and rear were adorned with gird-
er-like bumpers that often stood inches away from the
body and free-standing headlights were bolted on like a
hand-me-down from the days when cars were lit by oil lamps.
In creating the Y-Job, Earl took the dramatic step of throwing
out the styling rulebook and started from scratch using the best
tool that a designer could ever possess – his imagination. Assisted
by the unparalleled styling skills of George Snyder and the technical
expertise of Buick's Chief Engineer Charlie Chayne he created a stun-
ningly beautiful streamlined two-seater in the sports grand touring tradi-
tion. It was a colossal in size, measures 208-in. (529 cm in length (almost
3.9-in/10 cm longer than a contemporary LWB S-Class Mercedes Benz) and
74.4 in. (189 cm) wide, but stood just 57.8 in. (147 cm) to the top of its gor-
geously raked split windscreen thanks to the hitherto unheard of use of specially made 13-in (33-cm) rims. Gone were the running boards and perpendicular
styling. In its place were aerodynamic tapering fenders complete with power-oper-

ated concealed headlamps that flowed seamlessly into doors fitted with flush handles and the world's first electric windows. To the rear, recessed tail-lamps and a pop-out boot handle accentuated its sleek lines. Aside from the outstanding design the Y-Job's pièce de résistance was, undoubtedly its power-operated convertible hood that folded away into a hidden metal boot – a design that was later copied by Ford and has influenced car design ever since. And that is the purpose of the concept car – to offer a glimpse into the future and to demonstrate what can be made possible.

Hardly any concept car designs ever see the light of day as a full production automobile – there are, of course, exceptions but these are relatively few and far between. But that is not the point. The concept car can offer a designer or manufacturer a rare artistic freedom unbound by the shackles of practicality. It can act as a platform to demonstrate new technologies in engineering and manufacturing. If can show how new, cleaner, sustainable fuel sources could be used in the future. Above all, it call allow us to dream, to hope and, in the words of H.G. Wells, see "the shape of things to come."

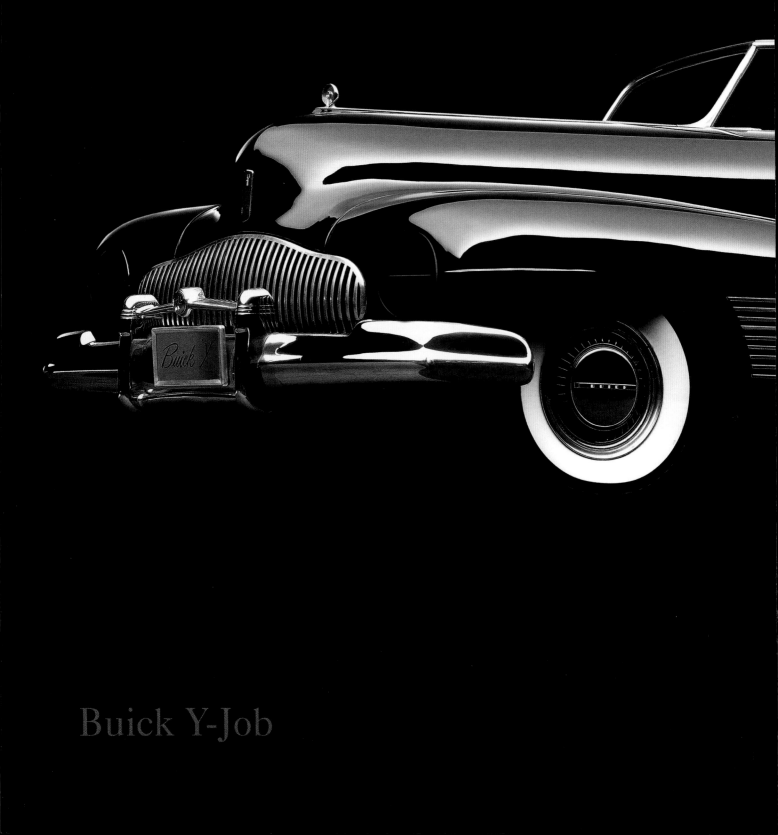

Buick Y-Job

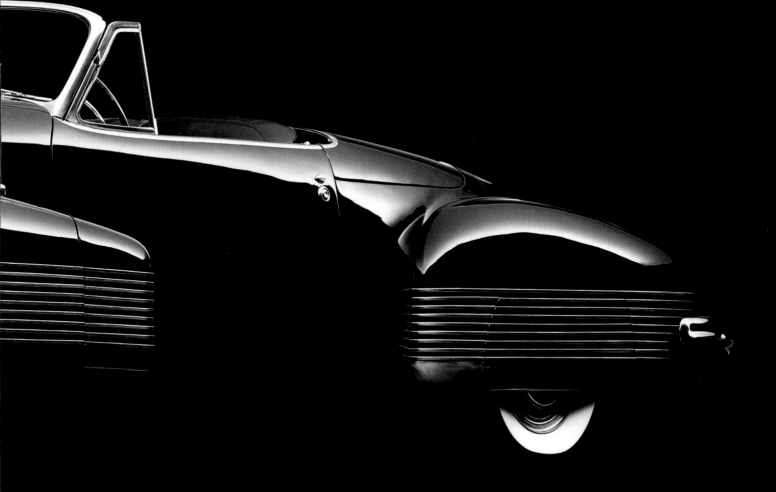

a new benchmark in car design

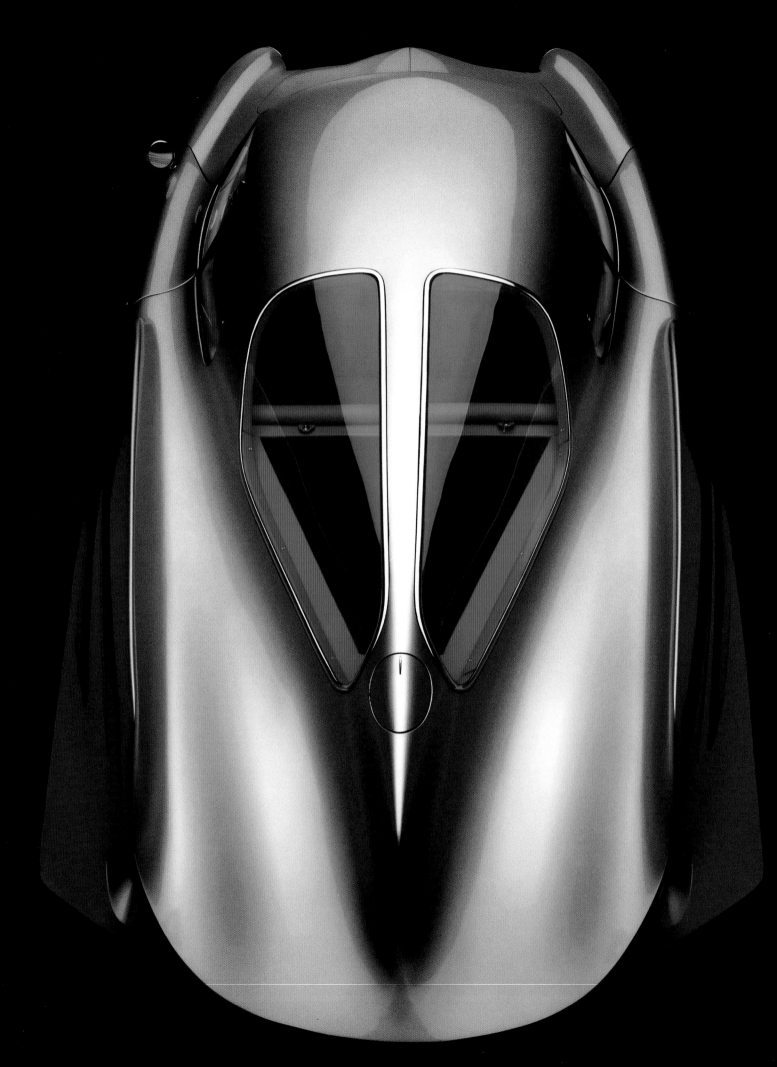

a brave new world
pre-1965

CHAPTER 1

12 The super-slippery B.A.T. 9's enormous rear fins display some of the most avant-garde automotive styling ever seen.

Although Harley Earl's Buick Y-Job set a new precedent in the world of car design, circumstances prevented the up-and-coming motor industry from capitalizing on its fame. The advent of the Second World War had a crippling effect on car manufacturing across the globe as raw materials, factories, and expertise were concentrated on the war effort and tanks, aircraft, and munitions rolled off the production lines.

With the cessation of hostilities in 1945, nations slowly but surely started to piece themselves back together with a new feeling of hope spreading far and wide. The war had given birth to new technology: the jet engine and the rocket were now a reality; clumsy and fragile wood and fabric aircraft had been replaced by sleek new aluminium machines that were fast, manoeuvrable, and aerodynamic; and, crucially, the world had entered a nuclear age. It was an exciting time when anything seemed possible – a maxim not lost on the car designers of the time.

One of the first to capitalize on this burgeoning culture of change was Earl himself. If the Y-Job had successfully echoed the glitz and glamor of Hollywood's Sunset Boulevard, then his next concept was a chrome-laden celebration of the jet fighter. His 1951 General Motors LeSabre was dubbed "an experimental laboratory on wheels" with huge tail-fins, dual-fuel technology, a spinning-disc speedometer, and even an altimeter. Several years later and, with the Space Race in full swing, he took the idea a step further with his Firebird series of concept cars which not only took visual clues from the aerospace industry, but, in harnessing the power of the gas-turbine motor, utilized the technology as well.

As the North American car industry became a haze of ostentatious fins, Plexiglas windshields, and chrome, designers on the opposite side of the Atlantic were taking a very different approach. In 1947, Battista "Pinin" Farina penned the design for the Cisitalia 202, which is considered to this day to be one of the most outstanding, attractive, and influential vehicle designs of all time. Elegant, sweeping, and curvaceous like a naked female form its seamless design found no need for the brazen showmanship of its American cousins. Instead, it demonstrated how pure artistic splendour could be incorporated into functional design. Gimmick free, it was beauty personified – a sculpture on wheels – the automotive equivalent of Michelangelo's *David*.

Pininfarina was far from being the only car designer cutting his teeth in post-war Europe: Lorenzo Fioravanti was in his employ before joining Ferrari; a young Giorgio Giugiaro was finding his way as an apprentice with Fiat; and aeronautical engineering graduate Franco Scaglione was working for Bertone. Scaglione's designs also proved to be some of the most influential of the time. His series of B.A.T. car concepts produced between 1953 and 1955, whilst grossly avant-garde, were a miracle of aerodynamic efficiency and his racing orientated Alfa Romeo 2000 Sportiva was as elegant and graceful in its form as anything shown before or since.

The truth was that, through this proliferation of concept car design, automotive styling was coming of age. Stateside it was all about gadgets, gizmos, and technology, while in Europe it was led by artistry and passion. Both schools were, however, about to come together in an almighty wedge-shaped clash.

Battista "Pinin" Farina's outstanding
1947 creation, the Cisitalia 202

Cisitalia 202

Jaguar / SS

the prototype for the 1935 Jaguar SS

Bugatti / Aérolithe

Designed by Ettore Bugatti's talented son Jean,
the magnificent Aérolithe debuted
at the 1935 Paris show.
Its unique magnesium-derived Elektron
body was just one third of the weight
of the equivalent aluminium

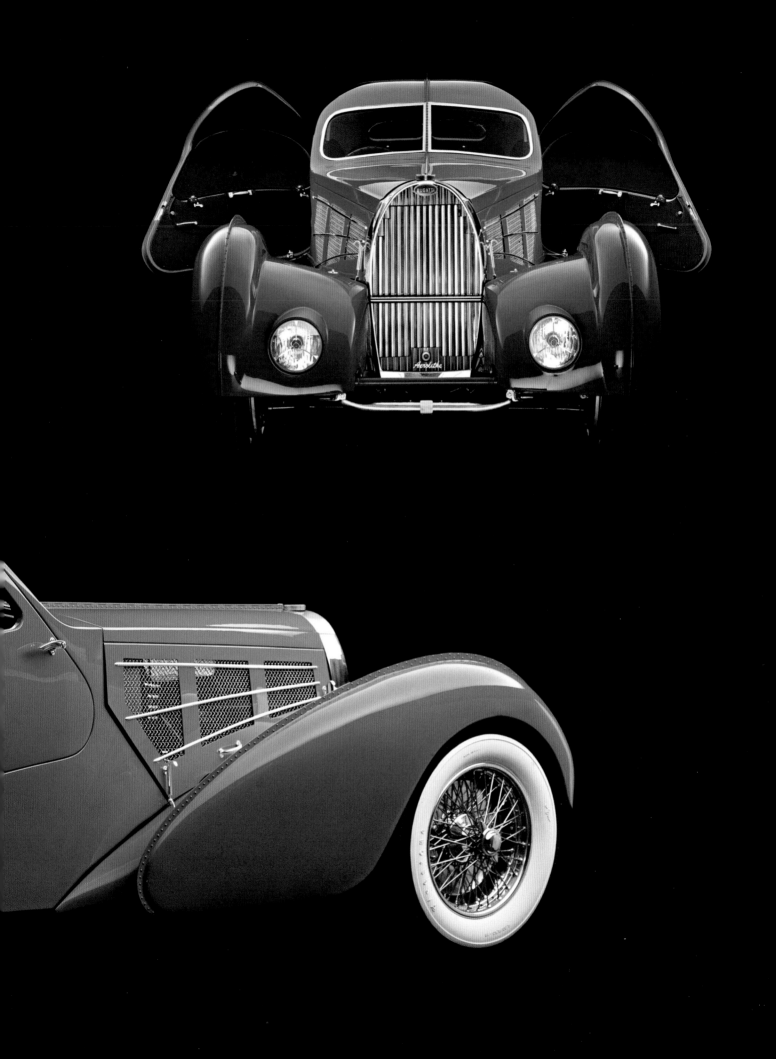

Airomobile / Sedan

1937

Paul Lewis created his Airomobile
as a cheap and practical sedan

24 From the front, the Lewis American Airways Airomobile
looks not unlike many other designs of the time.

25 From the rear the three wheel design becomes more
apparent particularly characterised by its unique fish tail.

Buick / LeSabre

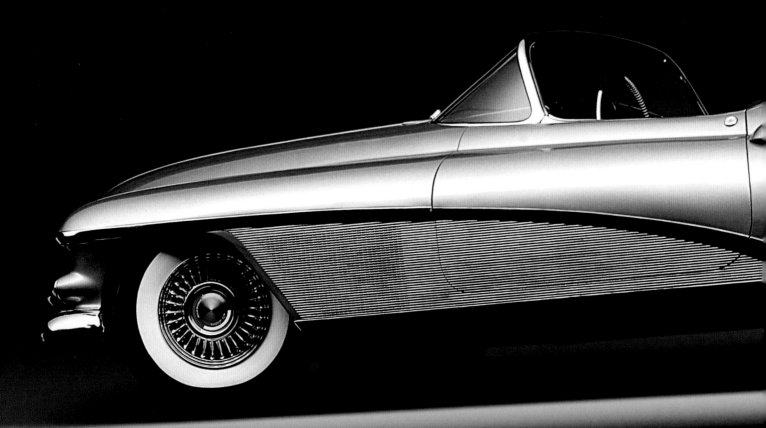

another creation from Harley Earl and
his team, the 1951 Buick LeSabre

Lancia / PF 200

Pininfarina transformed Lancia's
mundane Aurelia sedan with this
handsome 1953 Lancia PF200 concept

B.A.T. /5

1953

the B.A.T. 5 or the Batmobile?

B.A.T. /7

the bullet shaped B.A.T. 7 remains one of
the most aerodynamic designs of all time

1954

B.A.T. /9

1955

the B.A.T. 9: inspiration for the Alfa Romeo 2000

Alfa Romeo 2000 Sportiva

1954

Scaglione unveiled the motorsport orientated Alfa
Romeo 2000 Sportiva

Pontiac / Bonneville

the 1954 Pontiac Bonneville Special
is another Harley Earl creation

Chevrolet Nomad
Sport Wagon

styling ahead of its time, the Chevrolet Nomad

1955

Alfa Romeo
Giulietta Spider

Bertone's Giulietta Spider – the Alfa blueprint

GM/Firebird III

Harley Earl's – titanium skinned
Firebird III

IMAGINATION IN MOTION

INTRODUCING THE NEWEST GENERAL MOTORS
"LABORATORY ON WHEELS..."
AN AMAZING EXPERIENCE IN AUTOMATIC CAR CONTROL!

FIREBIRD III

1959

the wedge
from late 60s to late 80s

CHAPTER 2

American concept car design in the 1950s and '60s had been all about muscle and fins. At the same time in Europe, or at least Italy, design had been driven by elegant sweeping lines and aerodynamics. All of these cars had a wonderfully freehand feel to them as if every line had been penned in a single, fluid motion. They were graceful, classic, oozed passion and emotion and wholly reflected the newfound feeling of freedom and liberation that prevailed at the time.

With the arrival of the 1970s, an altogether different design philosophy took hold. Man had landed on the moon, in an instant converting science fiction into science fact, and we had seen the birth of the microprocessor and the computer. Car designers, meanwhile, had once again discovered the sharp edge and the straight line. One of the earliest concepts to display this new trend was the Bizzarrini Manta – a creation of the Italdesign Studio set up in the late 1960s by former Bertone and Ghia prodigy Giorgetto Giugiaro. Based on a Bizzarrini Le Mans racing chassis, it was powered by a 5.3-liter Chevrolet V8 mounted just behind the driver in a revolutionary mid-engine configuration which allowed the nose and windshield of the car to be raked back sharply at an incredible 15 degrees. Uniquely, it was a three-seater with the driver taking a central position with the steering wheel protruding from a low-slung dash that was located as far away as the pedals. Striking, futuristic and very, very different, this design was the first of the so-called Wedges that were to define the decade.

If Giugiaro's design for the Manta had served us the automotive hors d'œuvre for the decade, then Pininfarina dished up the main course with his dramatically radical Ferrari based Modulo. Still regarded as one of the most stunning concept cars of all time the Modulo was the brainchild of designer Paolo Martin who, himself, described it as "the craziest dream car in the world." Standing just 3.68-in (9.35-cm) to the top of its roof it was, at first, rejected by Battista Farina who was concerned that its space-age looks would receive negative reviews from the all-important press. But Martin persevered, creating a full-size mock-up in his own time from polystyrene blocks. His persistence paid off, the Modulo concept car was built and, from its first showing at the Geneva Motor Show in 1970, it was an instant hit, subsequently winning nearly two dozen international design awards. Although still highly prominent at the dawn of the 1980s the influence of the 'wedge' in concept car design was soon to be in decline – replaced, instead, by a new, hi-tech, slippery school of thought. Glass was used copiously as new technology allowed the material to be pressed and shaped into ever more complex forms without loosing visual clarity. Alternative power sources were considered with solar becoming a watchword of the day. Few of these cars became design icons in the same way that the Cisitalia had managed forty years before but they did, nevertheless, act as an important stepping-stone in automotive design for the future. The '90s were just around the corner and, all of a sudden, the studios were about to get their mojo back!

Serenissima Jet Competizione

a one-off creation of ex-Ferrari designer Alberto Massimino

Jaguar XJ13

designed to compete in the 1964 Le Mans

Pininfarina Sigma

designed by Paolo Martin, the Pininfarina Sigma was a Formula 1 safety concept car

Ferrari 512S
Berlinetta Speziale

built on a thoroughbred 312P racing
chassis, and created by Pininfarina, it was
the star of the 1969 Turin Auto Show

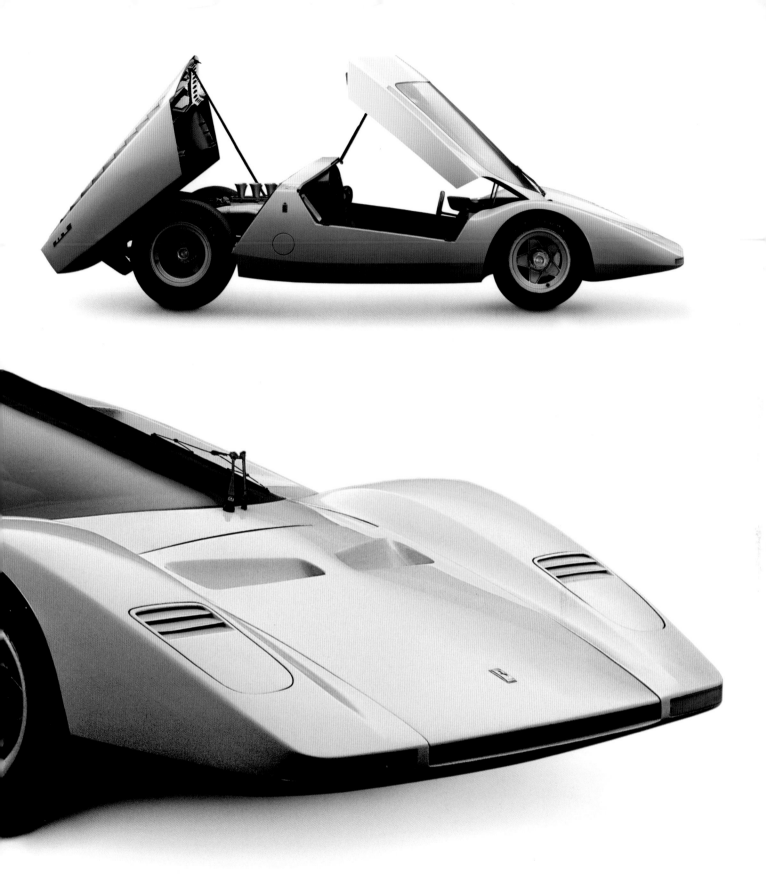

1969

Bizzarrini/Manta

1969

Giugiaro's Bizzarrini Manta was
created from scratch in just 40 days

Bertone / Stratos

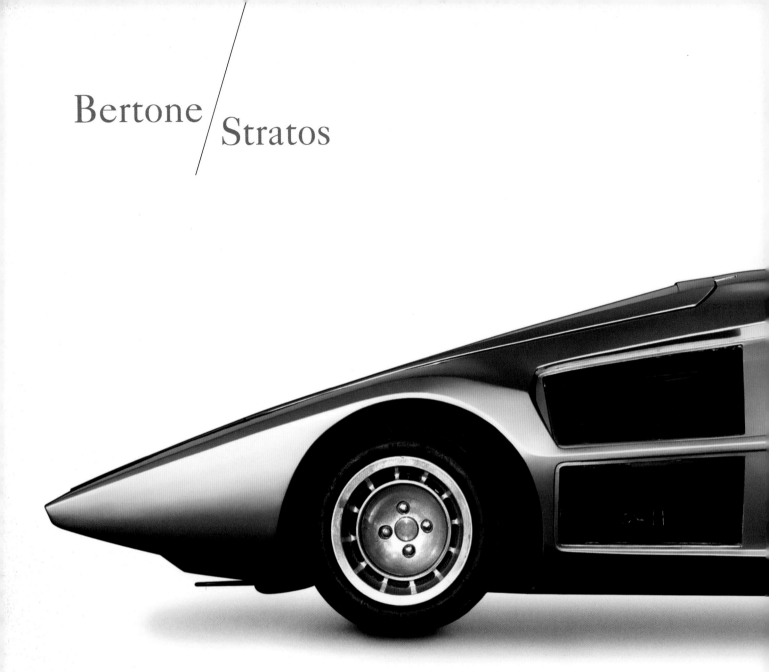

named Stratoline, it is credited as
having provided the inspiration
for the Lancia Stratos rally car

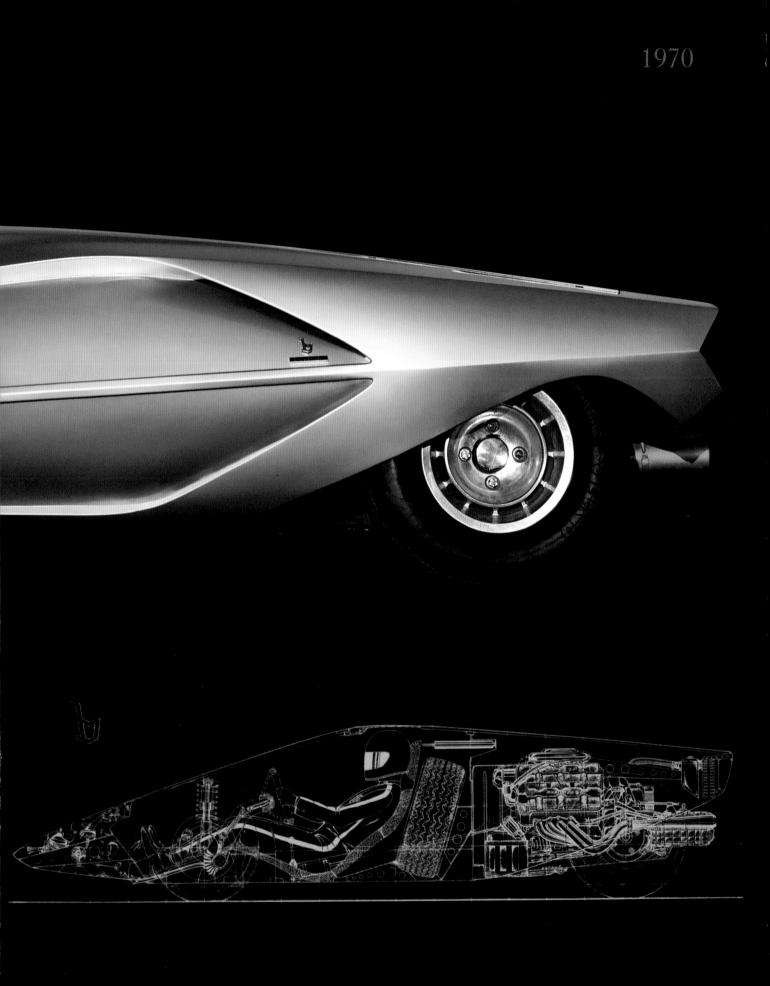

Ferrari / Modulo

Pininfarina's Ferrari Modulo concept
has earned 22 international awards

1985

Franco Sbarro
Challenge

the Porsche-based Sbarro Challenge
debuted at the 1985 Geneva Show

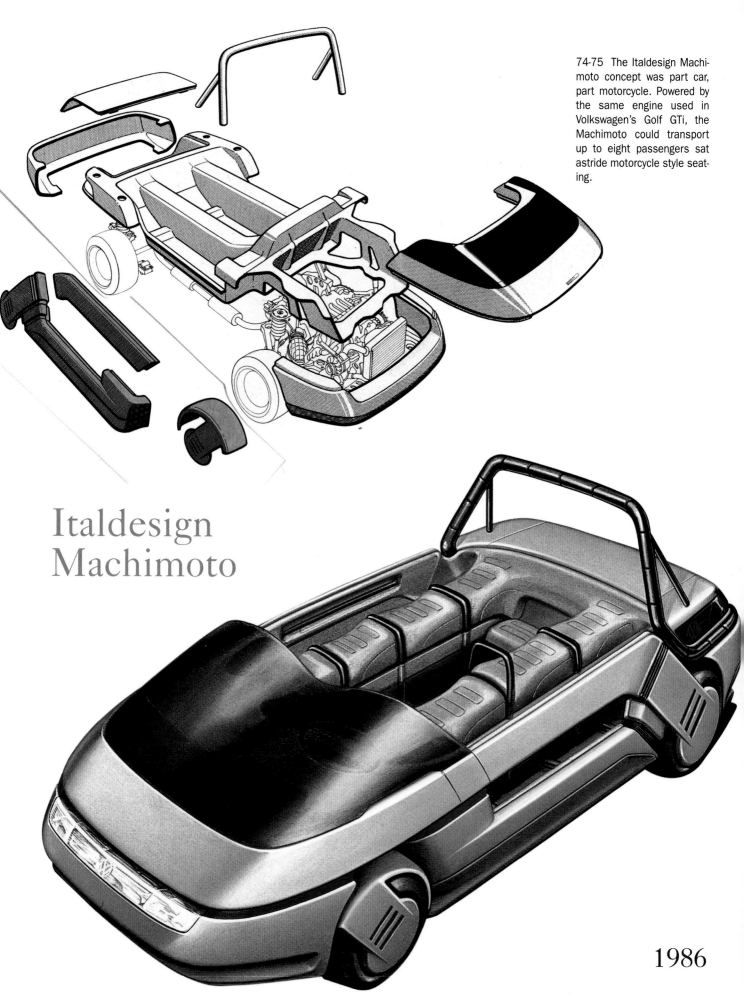

74-75 The Italdesign Machimoto concept was part car, part motorcycle. Powered by the same engine used in Volkswagen's Golf GTi, the Machimoto could transport up to eight passengers sat astride motorcycle style seating.

Italdesign
Machimoto

1986

fun, lightweight and undeniably futuristic

ITALDESIGN

Italdesign Aztec

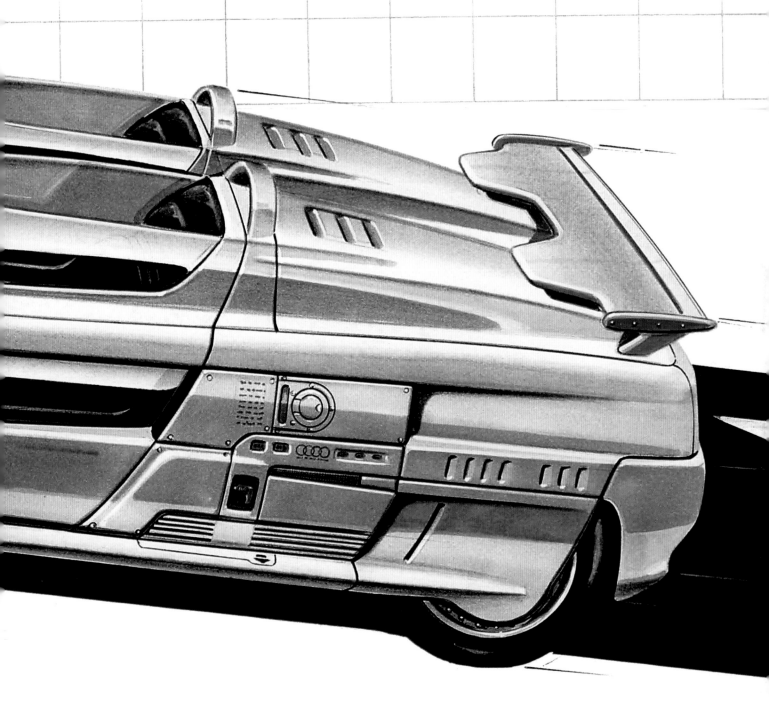

with its twin-cockpit design, this
is Giugiaro's most radical concept

Dodge / Viper

the impressive Dodge Viper RT710 developed as a modern interpretation of the muscle cars

breaking the mold
a return to grace
1990s to the turn of the millennium

CHAPTER 3

The beautiful 1995
Chrysler Atlantic concept
car started life as a hand
drawn sketch on a cocktail
napkin.

Good design can most certainly be indicative of an age but really great design never dates. The 1990s witnessed an impressive return to the graceful, fluid, retrospective styling of the past.

The straight edges of the wedge were cast away in favor of a new and exciting look that tipped a welcome hat to the masterful lines of the Alfa Sportiva, the Cisitalia and even Harley Earl's good old Buick Y-Job. In 1991, German manufacturer Audi pulled out all of the stops with its show-stopping Avus concept car – a spectacular polished-aluminum homage to the mighty Auto Unions that dominated the pre-war European racing scene. But the Avus demonstrated far more than just a creative bodywork design. For some time Audi had been working in partnership with ALCOA, the Aluminum Company of America, in the development of an all-aluminum production car. This was done with one clear aim in mind – a lighter car is a more economic car. Although the Avus was built as a non-running concept only – its impressive V12 engine, also in aluminum, was nothing more than a dummy – it set the stage not only for Audi's future product development but also raised questions of sustainability across the entire industry. In the United States the 1970s and '80s had been an arid time for concept-car design. There had, of course, been occasional moments of brilliance but the industry had suffered a torrid time in the wake of the oil crisis. However, the 1990s witnessed a return to greatness as

American manufacturers returned to the fray with a newfound air of confidence.

As with their European counterparts, retro design with a modern twist was the order of the day. It was once again time to celebrate the excesses of the 1950s and '60s – albeit with a little less chrome and slightly fewer tail-fins.

Nothing demonstrates this return to grace more than the now iconic Chrysler Atlantic – a design that is said to have originated as nothing more than a hand-drawn sketch on a hotel cocktail napkin.

As the Avus paid tribute to the thundering 1930s racers of Rosemeyer, Stuck and Varzi so the Atlantic offered reverence to the elegant hand-built coach work of the Bugatti Type-57 Atlantique and Talbot-Lago SS Coupe of the same period.

Sweeping curves were once again in fashion and the retro theme was carried through to an Art Deco styled interior and the use of a specially constructed straight-8 engine. Chrysler had wanted not only to turn heads with this exciting concept but to turn minds.

It is safe to say that they achieved both of their goals.

As the decade progressed the designs seen in concept cars just seemed to get better and better. The designers were on a roll – let loose with new materials, new techniques and, crucial new computer technology that pushed boundaries further than ever before. But the millennium was approaching and, with it, a whole new chapter in concept-car design.

Audi/Avus

1991

debuted at the 1991 Tokyo Show,
the Audi Avus sported a streamlined
lightweight all aluminium body

C for carbon fibre, 1000 for its horsepower

Mercedes Lotec C1000

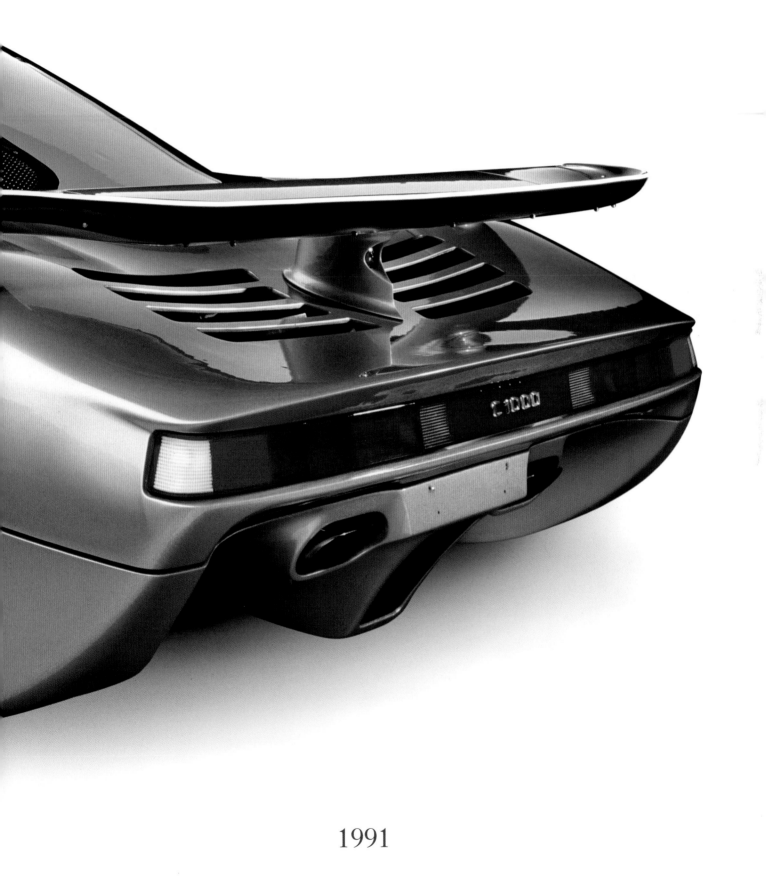

1991

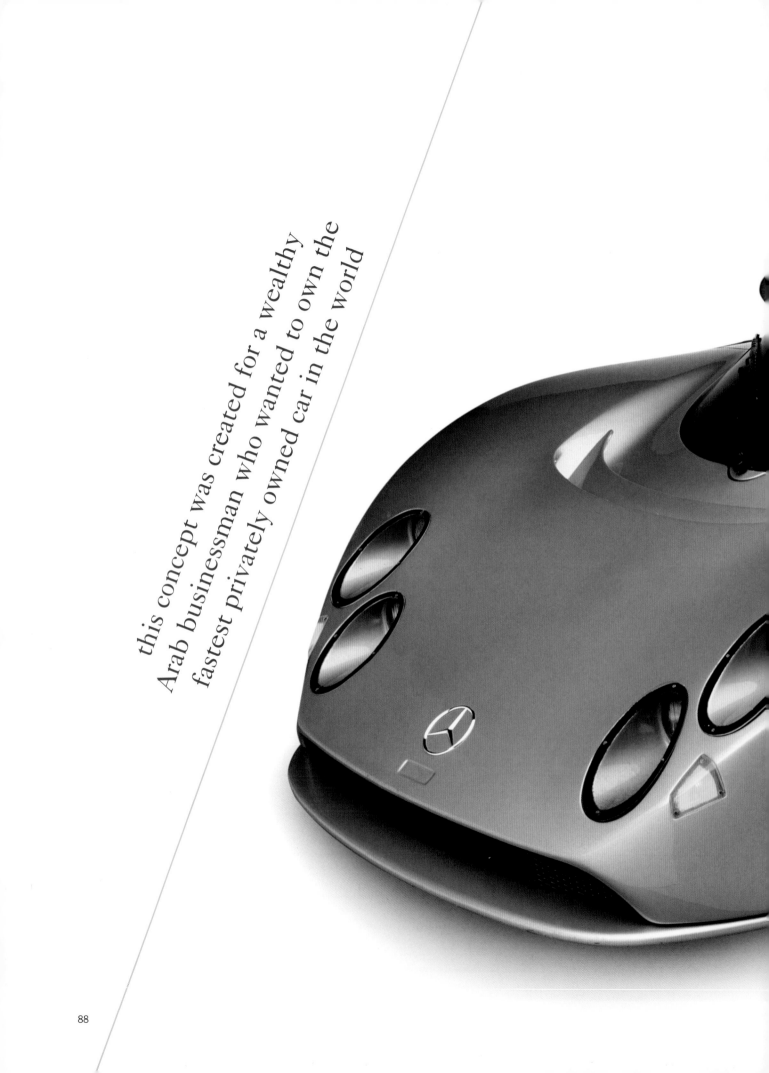

this concept was created for a wealthy Arab businessman who wanted to own the fastest privately owned car in the world

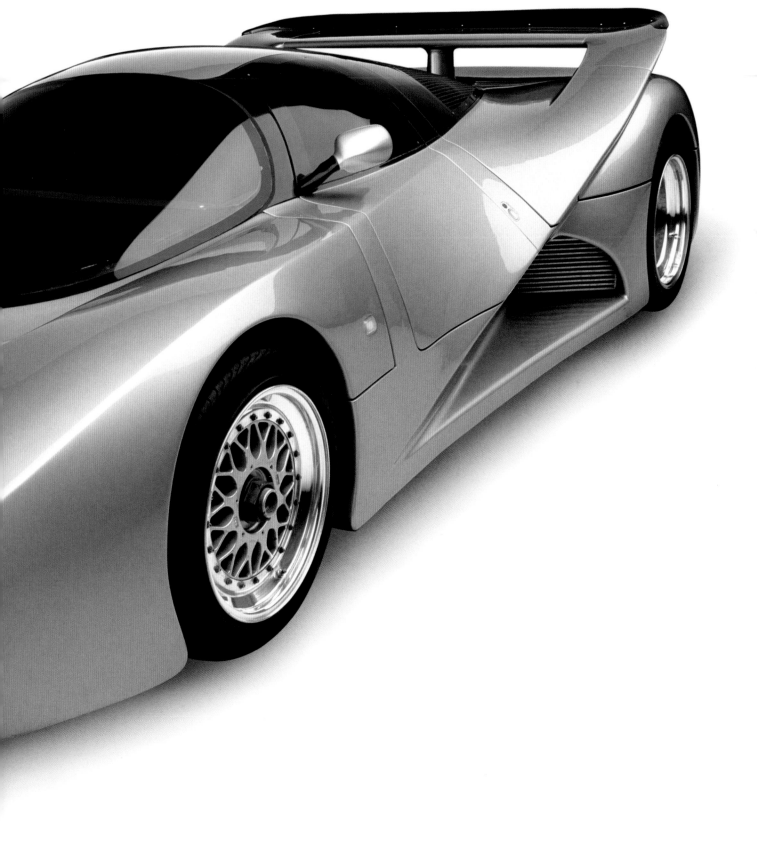

BMW / Nazca

1991

Giugiaro's 1991 Nazca C2 was one
of a trio of BMW-based concept cars

Plymouth / Prowler

1993

a healthy dose of retro styling

Bugatti
EB112

graceful, elegant and sleek – unmistakeable Bugatti

1993

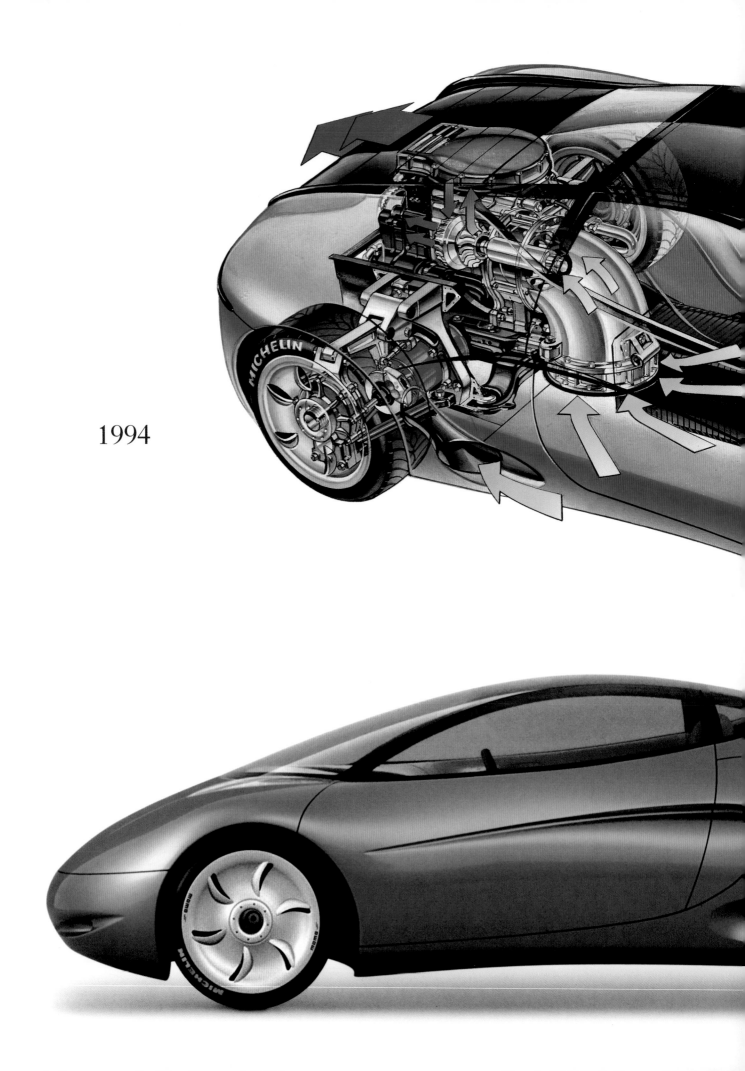

1994

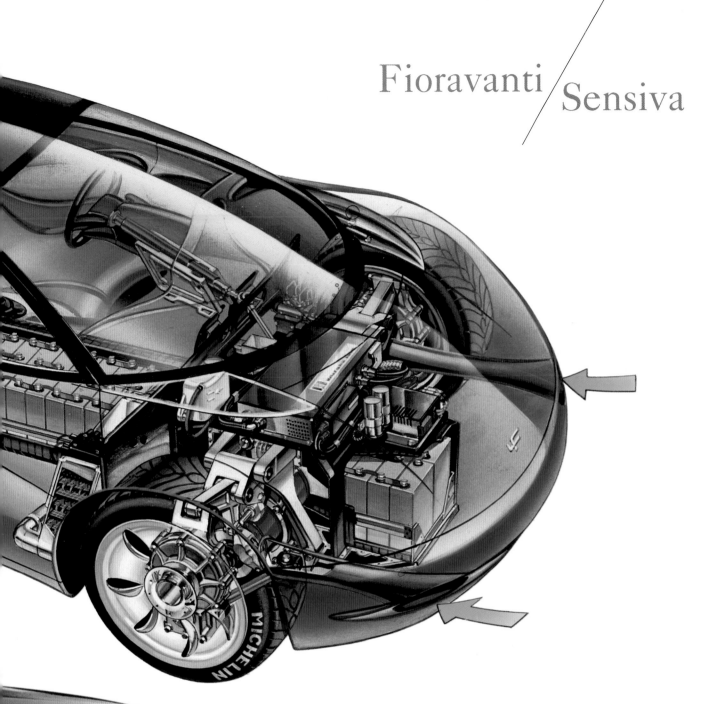

Fioravanti /Sensiva

an innovative
electric-hybrid

Ferrari / F50

1995

only three 750bhp Ferrari F50 GT
road-legal racers were ever produced

a fun packed roadster
from a traditional
master of understatement

BMW / Just 4/2

Chrysler / Atlantic

1995

an incredible rolling homage to the
custom coachbuilders of the 1930s

Lamborghini / Raptor

the Raptor by
Zagato debuted
at the 1996
Geneva show

simple and economic, the Fioravanti
Nyce demonstrated the concept
of the versatile compact SUV

Fioravanti Nyce

1996

Volkswagen /W12 Syncro

1997

the Giugiaro designed W12 was built
as a showpiece for the Volkswagen's
new 5.6 liter V12 engine

Alfa Romeo / Scighera

1997

a luxury car in race clothing by Giugiaro

Ferrari / F100

the F100 was built to celebrate
100 years since Enzo Ferrari's birth

1998

the XK180s design was influenced
by classic Jaguar racers

Matra P57

inspired by the classic Bugatti
Type 35 Racer of the 1920s

Cadillac EVOQ

1999

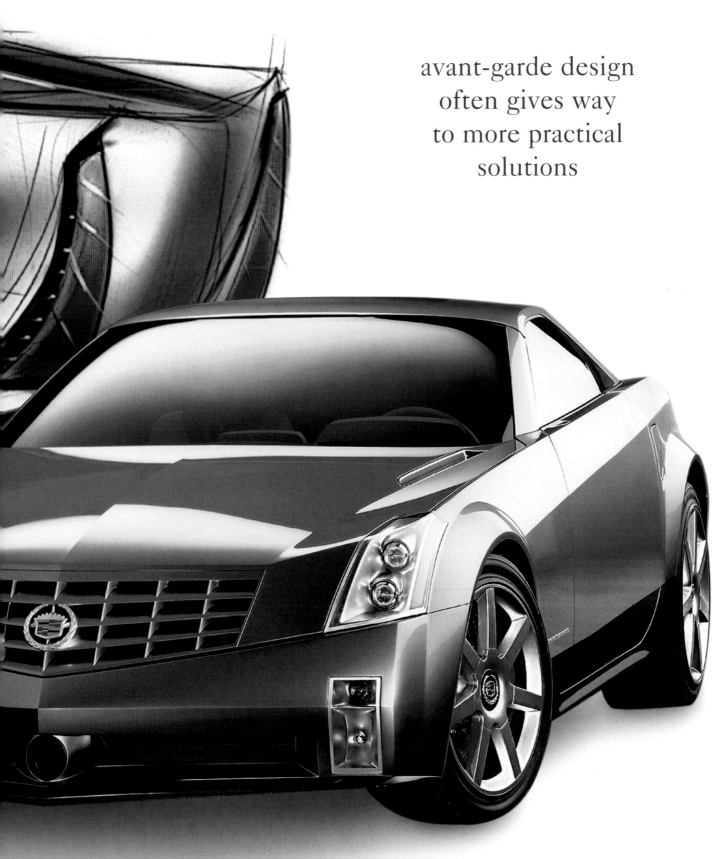

avant-garde design
often gives way
to more practical
solutions

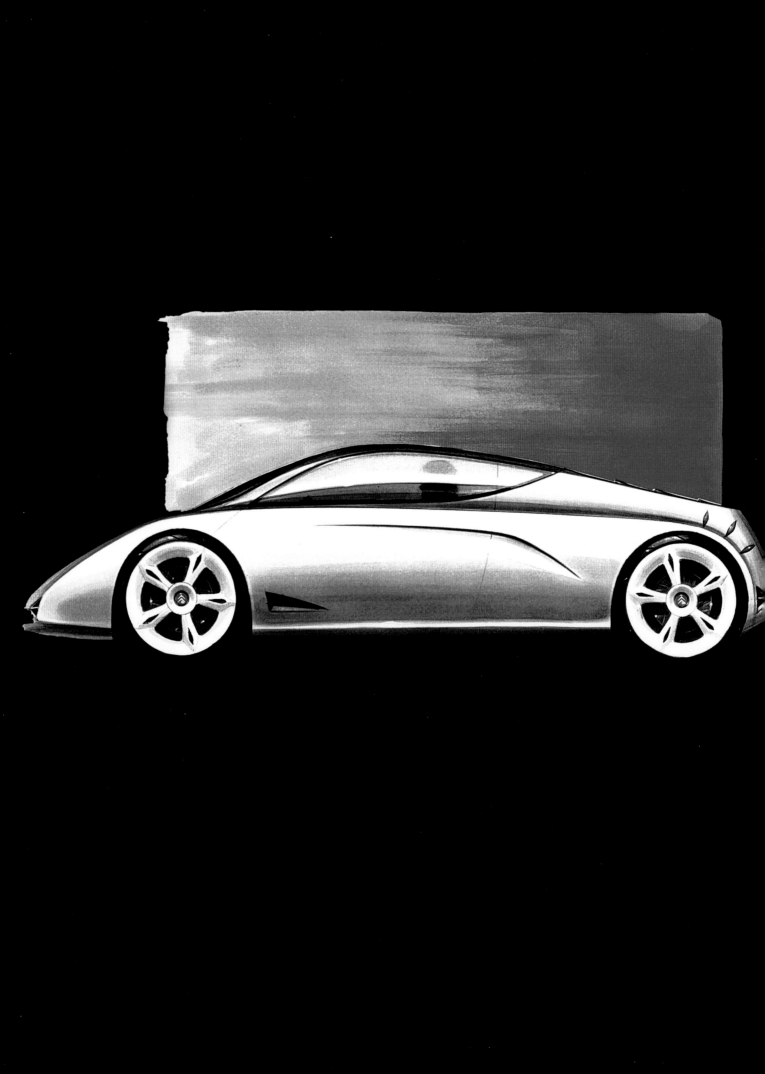

showing a little muscle
the "traditional" concept of the 2000s

CHAPTER 4

For a manufacturer or designer, one of the great things about creating a concept car is that it offers a rare opportunity to embrace truly free thought and to operate outside the usual design and cost parameters that hold a tight reign on the automotive industry. It is a very special opportunity to think outside of the box. Lateral thinking was very much in mind when Dodge created its Super 8 Hemi. This unique creation took styling cues from across a wide range of vehicle platforms – from rugged SUVs to traditional sedans – and threw in a liberal sprinkling of retrospective styling and state-of-the-art 21st-century technology.

Its wrap-around screen, front bench seat and sweeping roofline, for example, are pure 1950s while its dash incorporates a high-tech "Infotronic" system that offers the passengers online access to real-time traffic and weather updates, e-mail and internet access. Pininfarina, once more, showed characteristic inventiveness with its stunning mid-engine Citroën Osée. First shown at the prestigious Geneva Motor Show in 2001 it took the French manufacturer's iconic chevron logo as the key styling theme for both its exterior and interior. Shades of Giugiaro's Bizzarrini Manta can been seen in its 1+2 seating arrangement with passenger access gained via a hinged canopy rather than by traditional doors while rear visibility problems are resolved by use of a dash-mounted rear-facing CCTV system. In more recent years the prolific Italian design house has scored once again, this time with its unbelievable Maserati Birdcage 75th – a car described as "pure automotive fantasy" and "an uncompromised creation." Designed by Ken Okuyama, who also worked on the Osée as well as overseeing the creation of the Ferrari Enzo, its curious name paid homage both to Maserati's own classic Birdcage series of racing cars and Pininfarina's 75th anniversary but the design itself is anything but retrospective. Built on an all carbon-fiber chassis donated from a Maserati MC12 race car and powered by the same 6-liter V12 found in the Enzo, albeit tuned to 700 bhp, it was no shrinking violet.

The sweeping white bodywork, again constructed from carbon fiber, included a deep rear diffuser and a pair of active aero panels designed to automatically vary their height at speed to optimize down-force. Extending from nose to tail and dissecting the car in two is an incredible swathe of blue-tinted Perspex that not only provided the driver's canopy but also displayed the car's F1-style suspension and the carbon intakes of the mighty Ferrari power-plant. Sculpted sides gave the Birdcage a narrow profile and revealed the black carbon-fiber under-tray while its headlamp and taillight arrangement echoed the current line of production Maserati motors. There is no denying that the Birdcage's exterior was one of the boldest, most ambitious concept-car designs of all time but it was with the interior, and in particular the driver's controls, where this Maserati made its greatest statement. An F1-style steering wheel and center-mounted sequential gearbox were nothing new in that day and age but an innovative illuminated head-up display certainly was! Revs, speed, gear selection, even a traditional analog clock – all of the information usually provided by the dash instrumentation was projected onto a transparent screen in front of the driver. Perhaps the most incredible thing about the Birdcage 75th was the fact that it was built entirely from sustainable materials that emphasized the use of recycled components rather than just using natural resources.

Ferrari / Rossa

2000

celebrating 70 years of design

Buick / Blackhawk

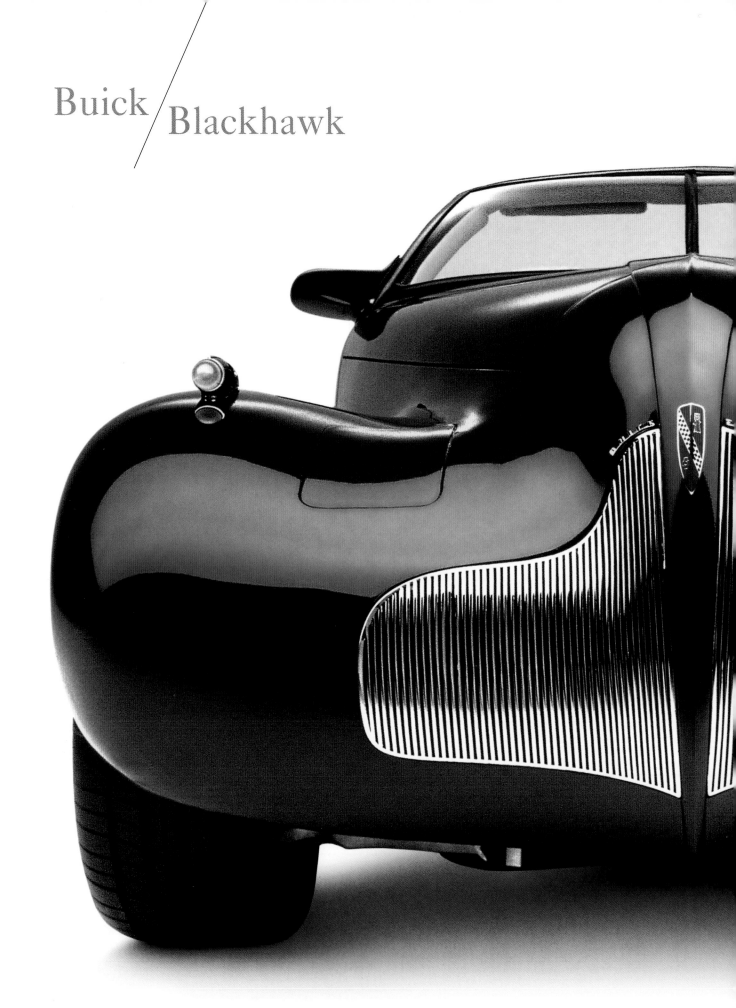

126

a Harley Earl Y-Job for the new millennium

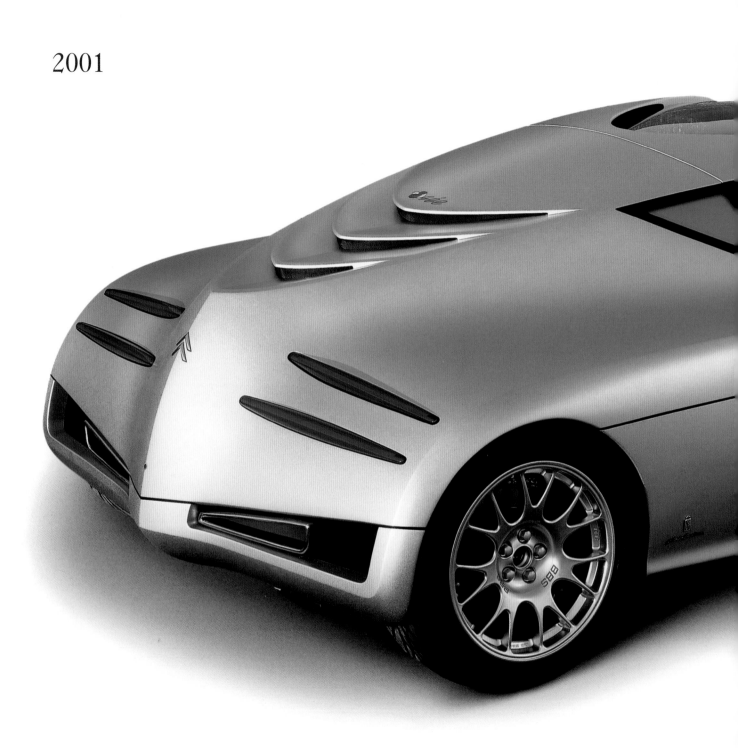

Pininfarina made clever use
of Citroën's chevron logo with
its design for the radical Osée

Citroën Osée

STRUMENTI SIMILI A
BINOCOLI

SCHERMO
TELECAMERA
RETROVISORE

costola
centrale

solido

solidi

C. BONZANIGO 09/2000

a compressed natural
gas/electric hybrid,
the Dodge Power Box
boasted near
zero emissions

Dodge
Power
Box

2001

Rinspeed
Advantage
R One

carbon design coupled with duel fuel technology

2001

Alfa Romeo / Brera

the Brera
Concept Car
of the Year 2002

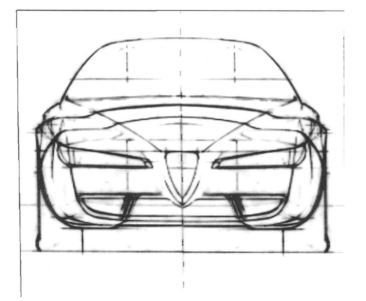

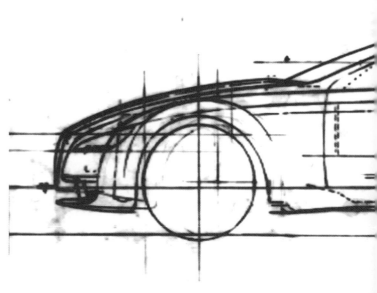

Cadillac/Cien

2002

designed and built
to celebrate Cadillac's
centenary – in England

Giugiaro's
V8-powered Kubang
SUV – luxury in
a tough package

Maserati Kubang

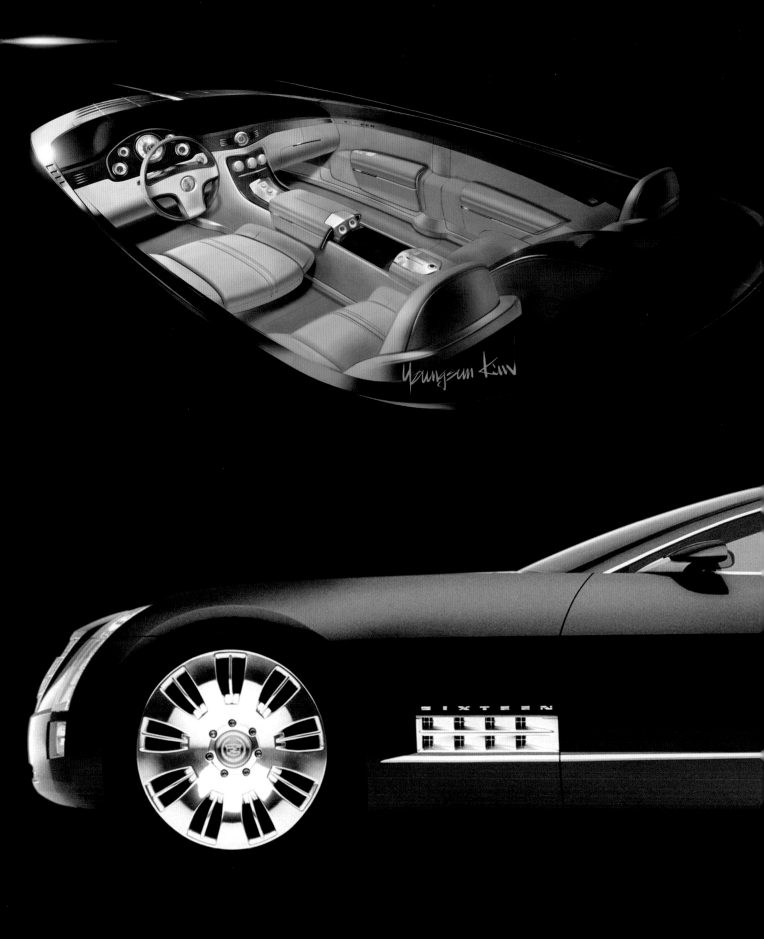

2003

Cadillac V Sixteen

1000 bhp from a 13.6 liter,
32 valve V16
the ultimate in excess

Ford Model U

2003

hydrogen powered technology

50 years of Corvette history in a single design

2003

Chevrolet Corvette

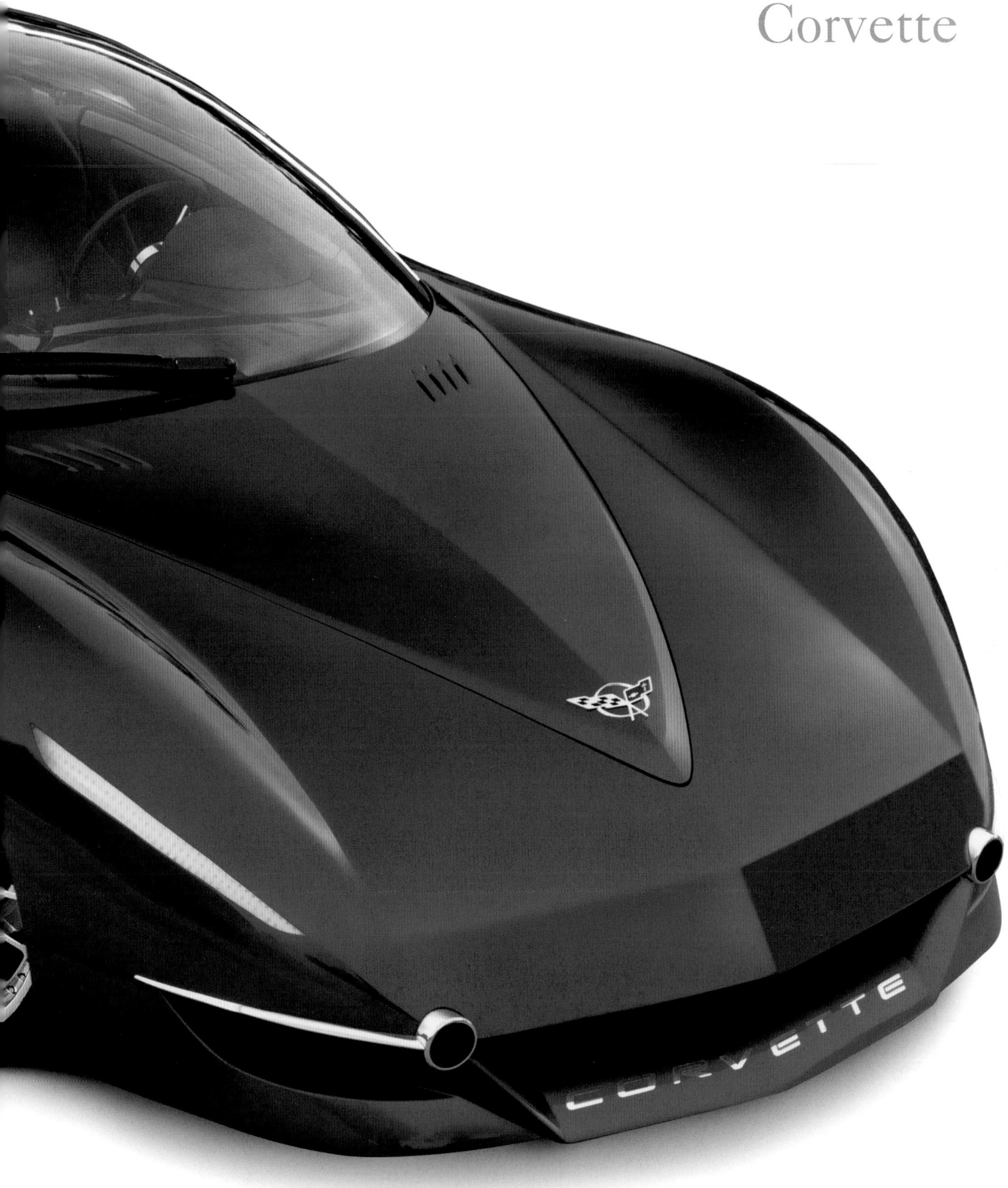

Chevrolet /ss

classic muscle car flavor
interpreted in a modern way

2003

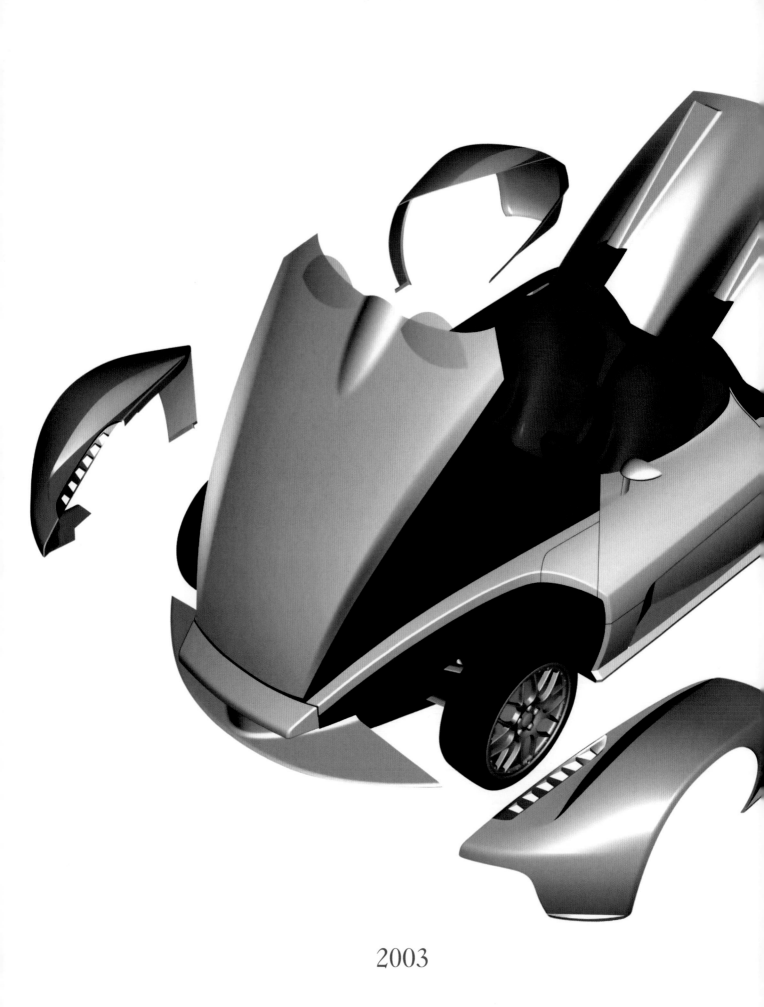

2003

Pininfarina Enjoy

the Lotus based Enjoy
features removable panels
that convert it into an
open wheeled track car

Chrysler / ME

2004

850bhp from a 6.0 liter V12
assisted by 4 turbochargers

2005

uncompromised and uninhibited,
the Birdcage is a car like no other

Cadillac / Villa

appropriately named, Bertone's
Cadillac Villa draws its influence
from contemporary architecture

2005

Audi / Shooting Brake

the Audi Shooting Brake explored the
idea of a TT derived sports estate car

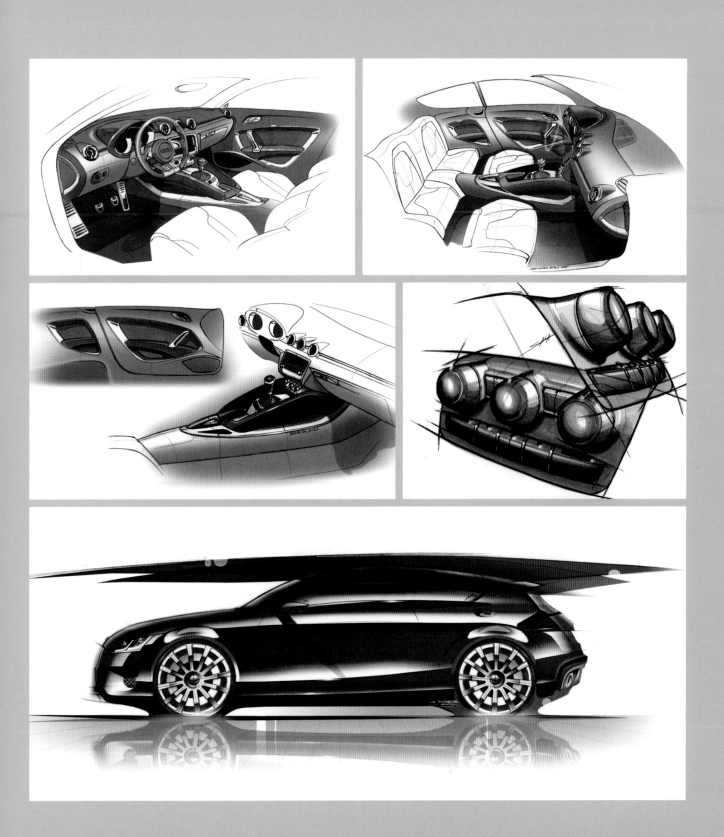

2005

BMW Mille Miglia

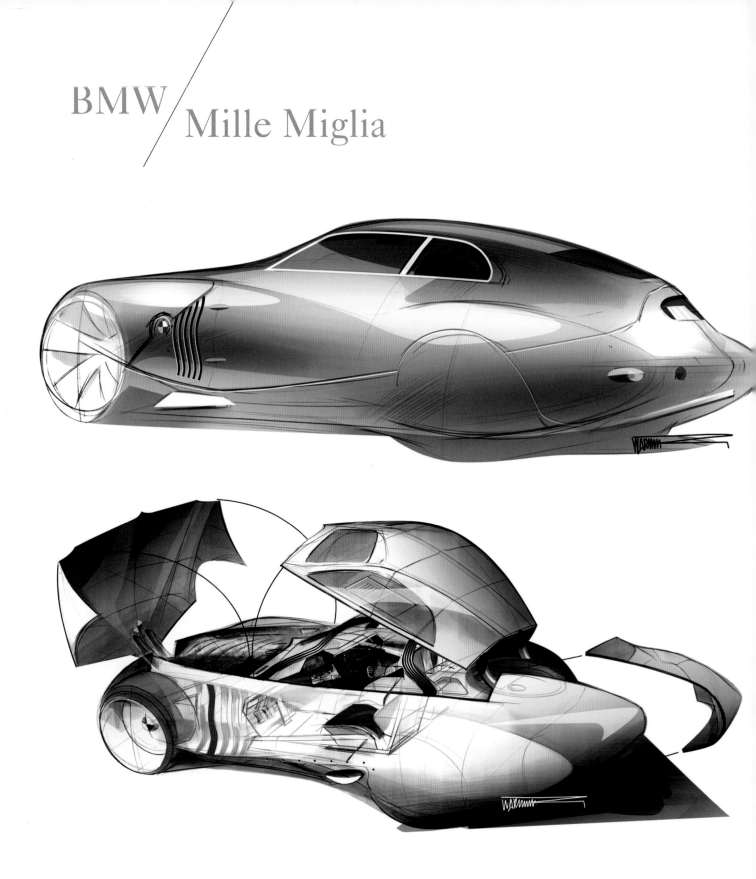

the Mille Miglia evokes the lines
of the great 1930s racers

2006

Bugatti Veyron

the name of this high performing luxury supercar took inspiration from the driver, Pierre Veyron, who won the 24 Hours of Le Mans in 1939

Ford GTX1

created by SVT designer Kip Ewing, the open air version of the Ford GT

Ferrari P4/5

based on the exclusive
Ferrari Enzo,
the unique P4/5 is
the ultimate supercar

2006

sharp looks and serious horsepower

Buick / Riviera

carbon fiber bodywork
and gull-wing doors
Harley Earl would be proud

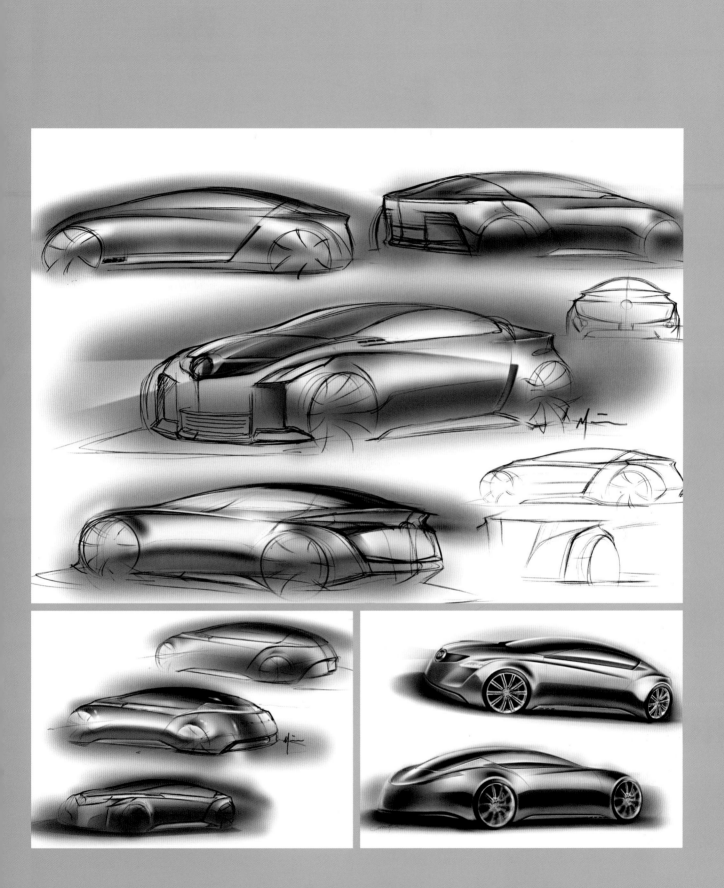

Mazda / Hakaze

Grand Touring excellence!

Chevrolet / Camaro

CAMARO

retro on the outside, high-tech on the inside

BMW/M1

BMW's dazzling
M1 Homage
combines the edgy
styling of
the 1978 original
with high-tech
modern detailing

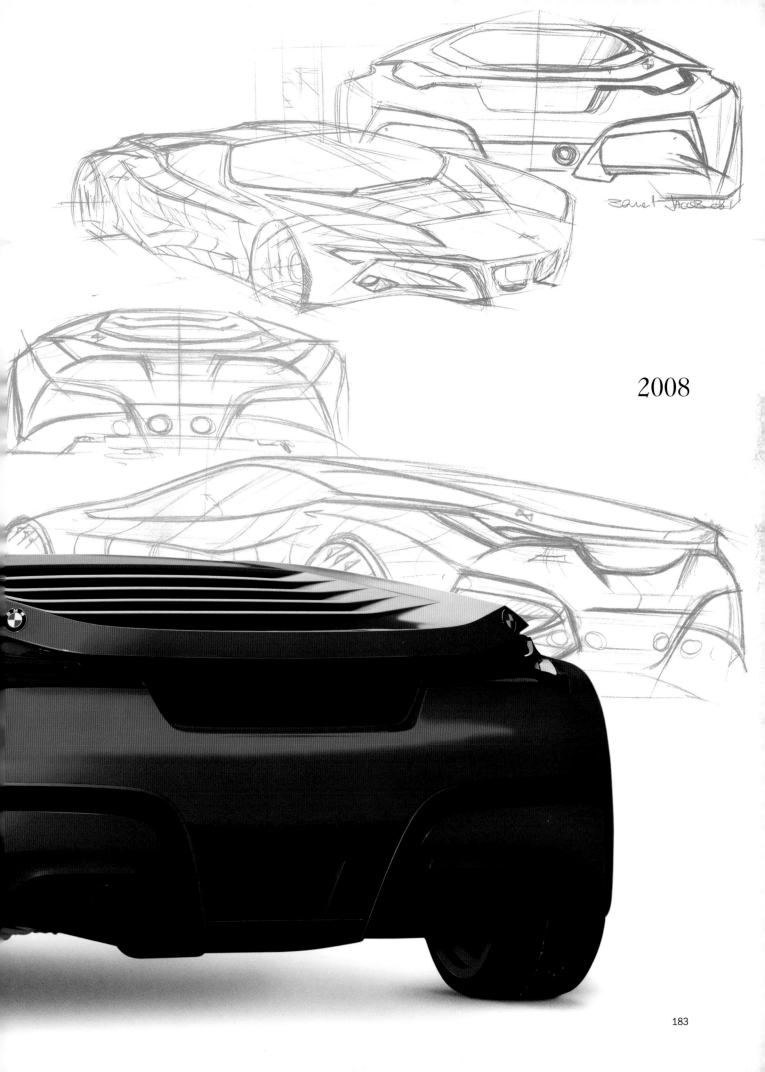

2008

Benoit Jacob 02/06

jaw dropping looks and
astonishing performance

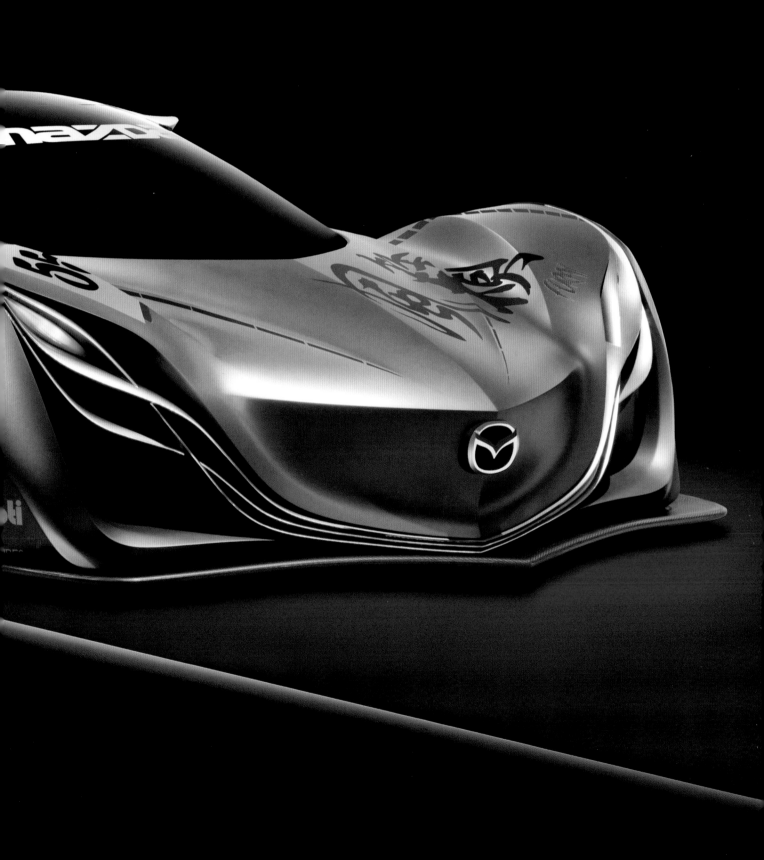

Mazda Furai

the Furai's design was inspired
by the movement of a kite's tail

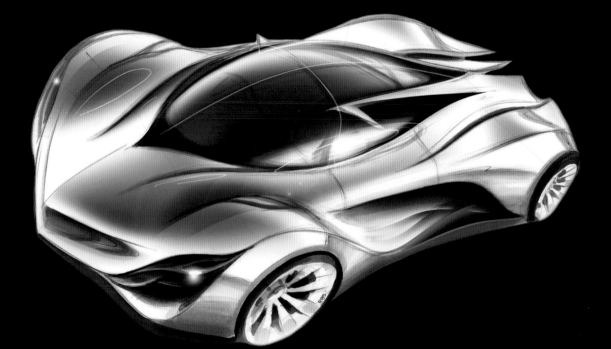

Furai

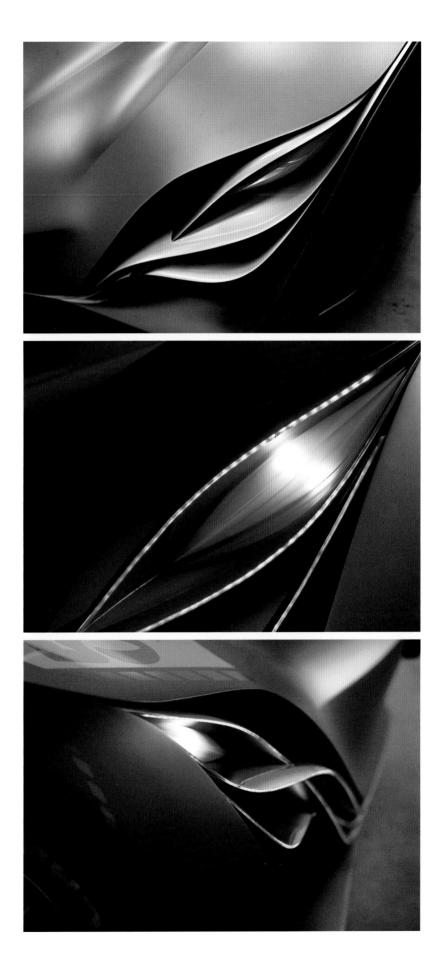

2008

Spyker C12 / Zagato

built to celebrate the company's
entry into Formula 1

2008

2008

V12 Diesel power gives a 0-100km/h in just 4.2 seconds

Dodge/Viper

2008

the astounding SRT-10 Mopar Concept

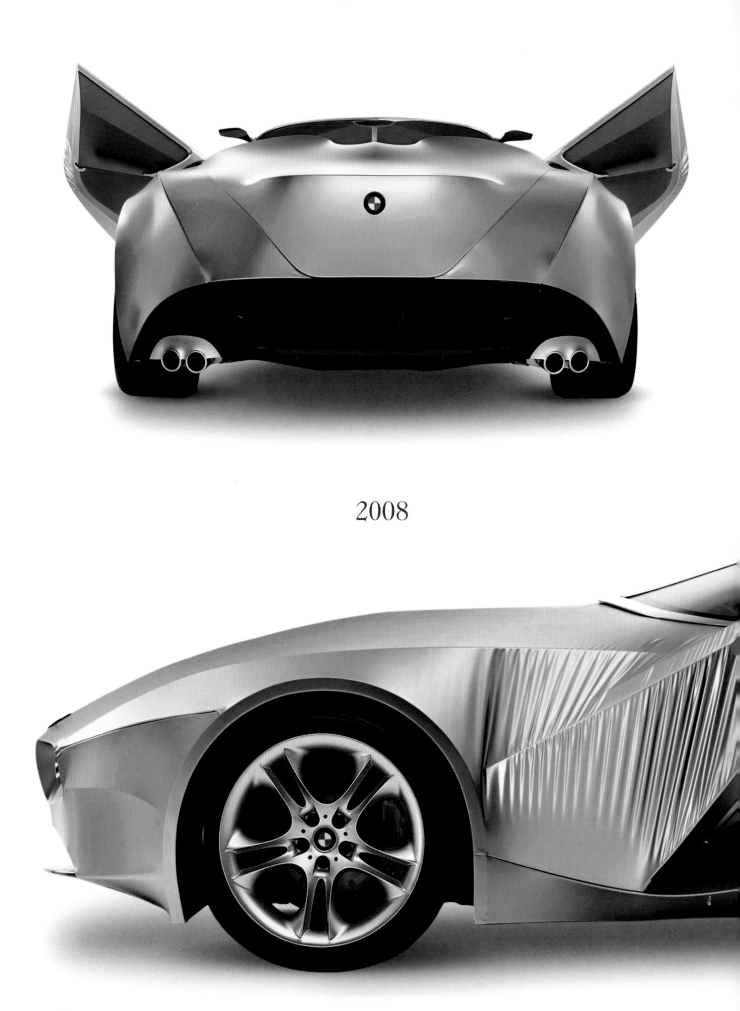

2008

BMW Gina

BMW's unique Gina
abandoned metal
bodywork in favor
of stretched fabric

Chevrolet Corvette Stingray

2009

built to commemorate the Chevrolet Corvette Stingray's
50th anniversary, and unveiled at the Dubai
International Motor Show, this concept car combined
the classical style lines of the Corvette with
the most innovative materials, technologies and design

Jaguar / C-X75

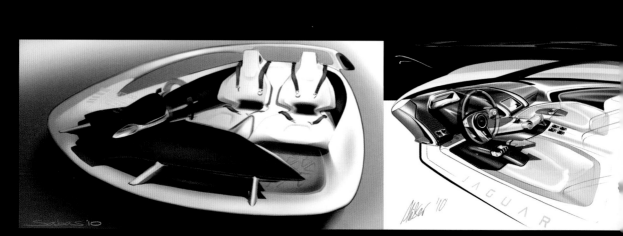

designed to celebrate Jaguar House's
75th anniversary, this sensational sporty coupè
was endowed with electric propulsion
and zero emissions

2010

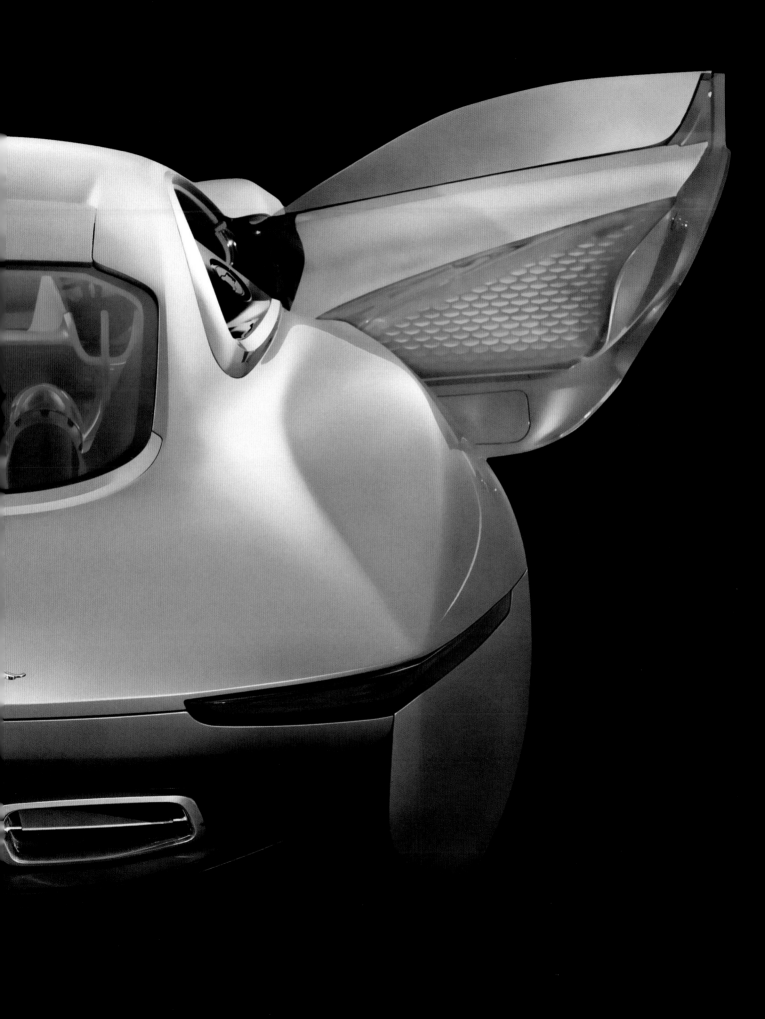

Alfa Romeo / 4C

presented as a concept
at the 2011 Geneva Motor Show,
this prototype of the Biscione House
entered production in 2012

2011

this dry two-seater is about 13.12 ft.
(4 meters) long, with a wheelbase
of less than 7.87 ft. (2.4 meters)

2011

BMW Vision
Connected Drive

more than a concept car, this two-seater
roadster is a show car, a technological demonstration
of developments in the field of ergonomics
and car-machine interaction.
This vision in fact is able to interact
with the ambience and communicate with the driver
thanks to a three-dimension display

Infiniti /Essence

2009

the Essence was presented at the 2009 Geneva
Motor Show commemorating the Infiniti's
twentieth anniversary

Peugeot Onyx

2012
the Peugeot's Onyx supercar debuted with spectacular
doors each made of a single sheet of pure copper and
a carbon fiber matte black body

the Ford Evos, according to J. Mays, Chief Creative Officer of the Ford group, is a "car designed not to provoke but to seduce"

Ford / Evos

2012

Honda / NSX

the Japanese Acura NSX sportscar, which is to be assembled in the United States, is pure elegance with environmental dynamism for a new all-wheel driving experience

BMW / i8

the BMW i8 is the most innovative sports car of this period with a hybrid electric motor interacting with the high combustion Sportiva 223 hp engine

2012

BMW i8 Concept

Lexus LF-CC

sinuous lines and flowy curves are the symbol
of this new Lexus LF-CC Concept

McLaren / X-1

commissioned by an anonymous wealthy collector, the McLaren X-1 Concept design was led by Design Director Frank Stephenson who was tasked with creating a car of "timeless and classical elegance"

2012

the Ferrari Sergio Concept, built as a tribute
to Sergio Pininfarina, is a two-seater
barchetta using exclusivity, innovation
and extreme lines

2013

Pininfarina / Sergio

designing for the future
the "nuclear family"

CHAPTER 5

228 The friendly little
Pivo2.

In the 21st century eco-issues have become more important for all of us. Today's watchwords are recycling, sustainability, economy and non-polluting – terms which, in the past, have sent fear into the hearts of car manufacturers the world over. On the whole, production vehicles are only just beginning to embrace the ideals of "green-living," but the automotive industry is doing far more than just sitting on its laurels. These issues have led to a deluge of new environmentally-aware concept cars gracing the halls of the usually high-octane international motor shows with each design attempting to tackle a new or different problem and, unsurprisingly, with Japan at the forefront of this pioneering revolution.

Nissan's Pivo2 was one of the most innovative of these designs. Created as an environmentally friendly electric urban commuter it may have looked like a space-helmet on a roller-skate but, in actual fact, concealed some wonderfully clever technology. Rather than using a central motor within the body, each wheel was powered by its own high-power, thin disk-shaped traction motor resulting in substantial space gains. Each wheel unit could be controlled independently for speed and direction which, coupled with the Pivo2's 360-degree revolving cabin, allowed the car to be driven sideways – avoiding the need for parallel parking in an instant. Perhaps the Pivo2's most endearing feature was its aptly named Robotic Agent – a cheery little fellow whose face peered over the instrument panel and interacts with the driver through conversation and facial gestures offering everything from navigational advice to soothing chat.

On similar lines, Toyota's expressive little 2001 POD concept also took on the issues surrounding commuter driving. One of the most amusing designs of all time, this diminutive little urban runabout welcomed you with a cheerful orange smile provided by a bank of yellow LEDs while poor driving and hard braking would result in a similar display of angry red lights!

The POD may not be the ultimate answer to global warming but it certainly helped to highlight that a happy driver is usually a better driver! Alternative-fuel sources are, without a doubt, the future of motoring and are always going to make headlines in the automotive world. There is, however, no reason to think that we will all be forced to drive around in faceless creations like the Toyota Prius. Ford has brought us its amazing and radical Airstream – an adventure-recreational vehicle powered by a plug-in hydrogen fuel-cell system that operated under electrical power at all time and could function in the dead of winter when similar systems were prone to fail.

Dodge created the Zeo – an electrically powered 2+2 sport wagon capable of hitting 0-62 mph (0-100 kmh) in less than 6 seconds. Even the normally sedate Swedish manufacturer Saab got in on the act in grand fashion with its astonishing Aero X.

Powered by a 2.8 liter twin-turbo V6 it produced in excess of 400 bhp and could battle its way to 62 mph (100 kmh) from a standstill in less than 5 seconds – a pretty amazing achievement for a car running on bio-fuel.

With exciting concept-car deigns such as these, "the shape of things to come" looks more promising than ever. Harley Earl would be proud!

Saab AeroX

the four-wheel drive Saab AeroX
was designed to run on pure ethanol

the partnership
between Toyota and Sony
resulted in this concept car
which enhanced
driver-car communication

Toyota
POD

2001

the friendly little car that always lets you know how it's feeling

Venturi/Fetish

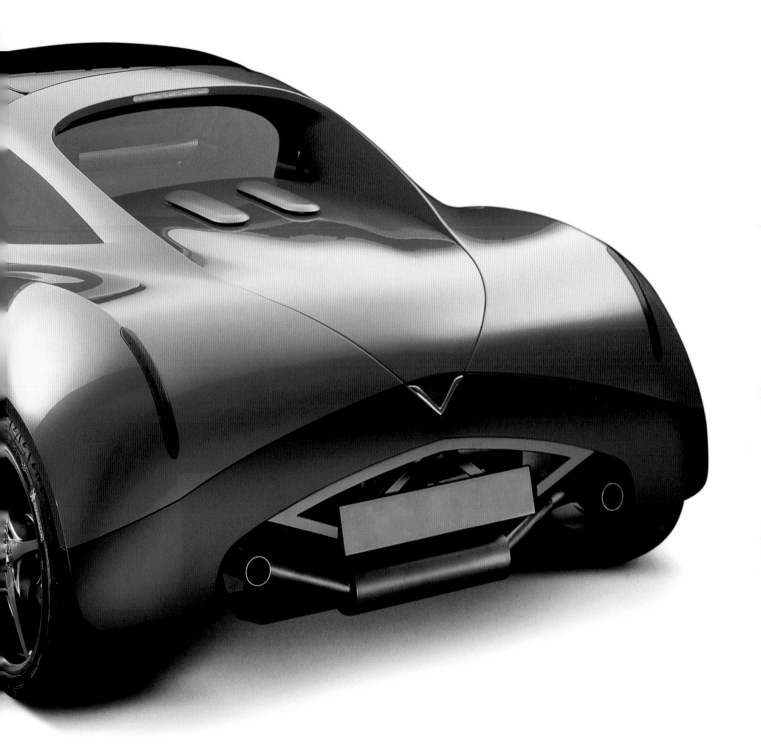

designed by Sacha Lakic,
the electric-powered carbon fibre
Venturi Fetish debuted
at the 2002 Geneva show

Citroën / C-Airdream

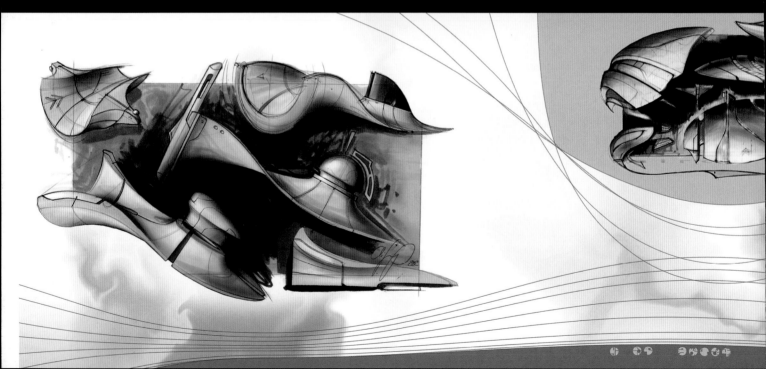

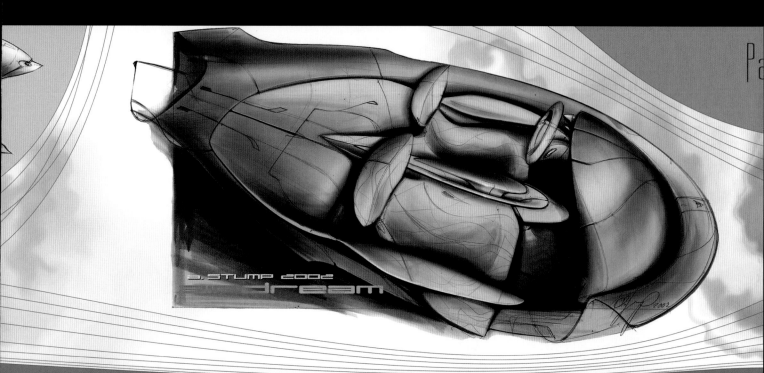

b.STUMP 2002
dream

our dream

malual 01

GM AUTOnomy

2002

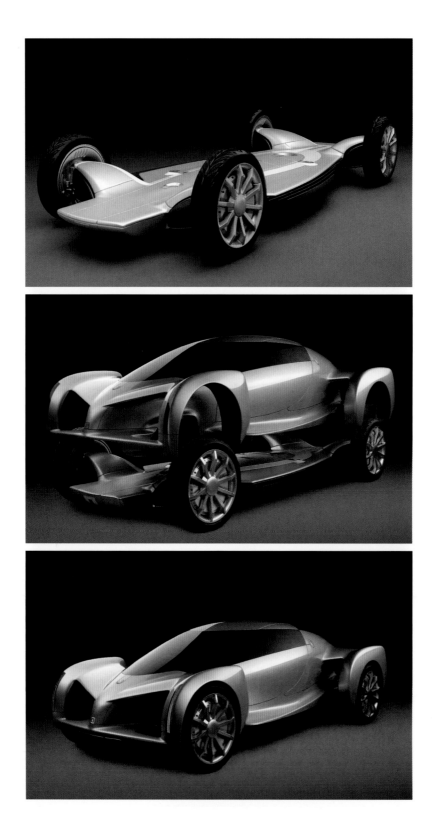

fuel cell technology, fly-by-wire controls
and a unique skateboard chassis

Nissan/Pivo

a rotating compartment
makes for simple
parking and easy access

2005

Ford / iosis X

Ford described the iosis X as
"energy in motion"

2006

Mazda / Nagare

2006

almost organic
in appearance

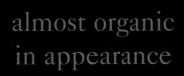

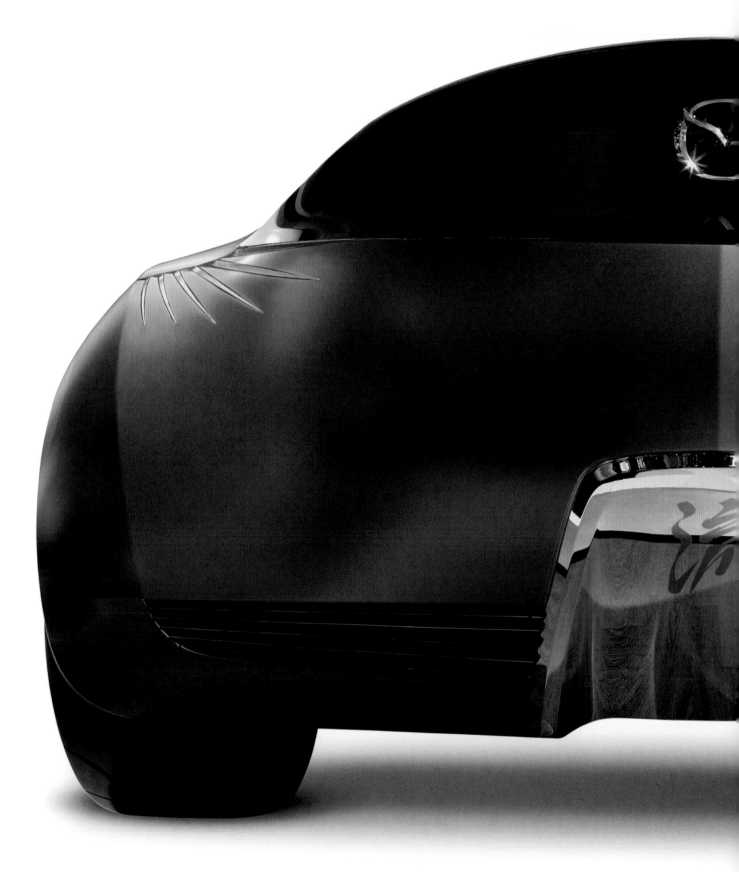

Nagare – Japanese for the embodiment of motion

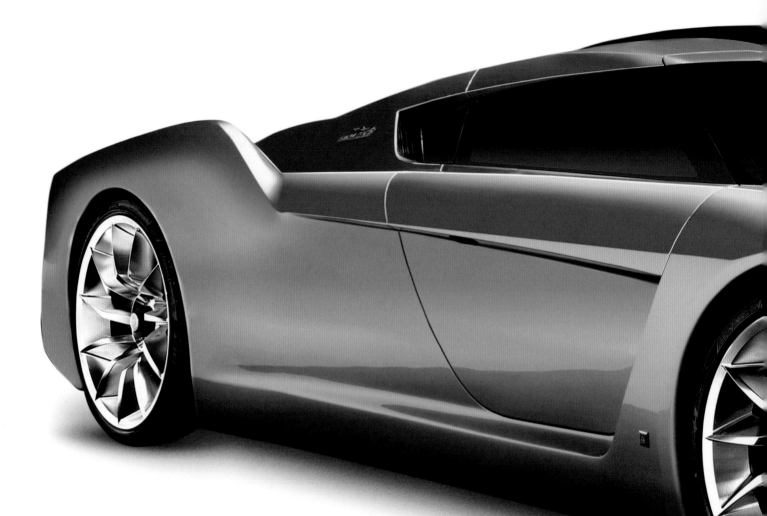

its powerplant is a biodiesel
powered jet turbine

General Motors Ecojet

2006

Alé Fuel Vapor

2006

running on fuel vapor,
the Alé achieves an amazing
2.56 liters/100 km (92 mpg)

Mazda / Taiki

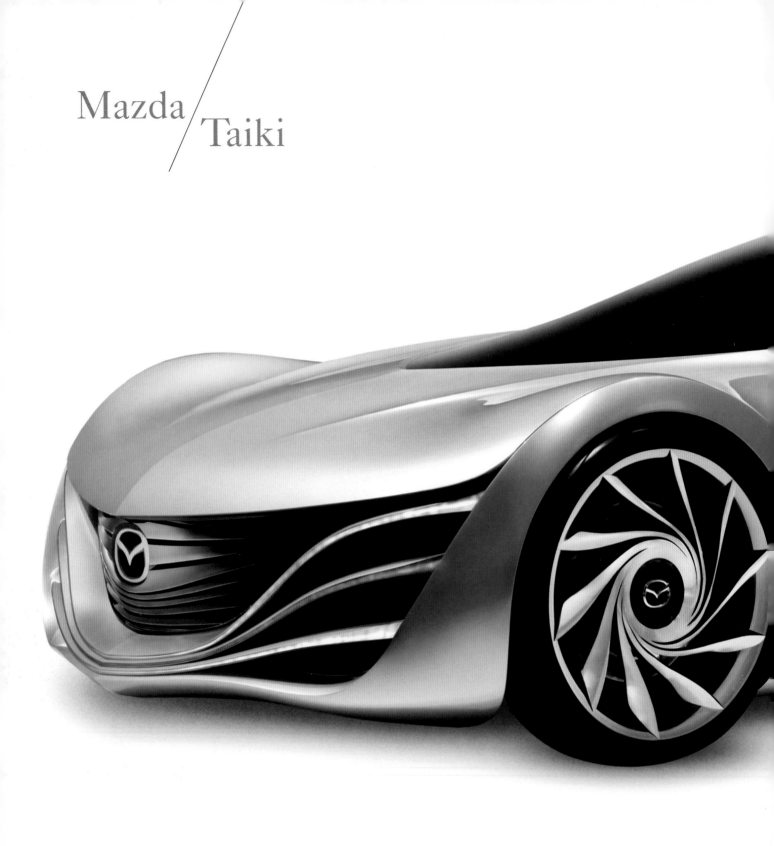

2007

aerodynamic, fuel efficient
and stunning to look at

Italdesign / Vadho

with no steering wheel the Vadho
is controlled using two joysticks

2007

Fioravanti /Thalía

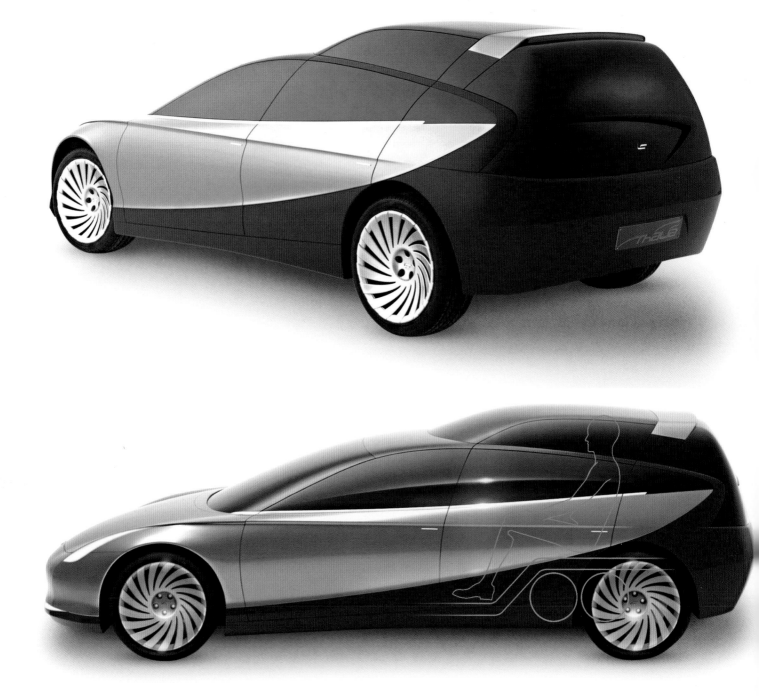

the raised rear seats of the Thalía
house hydrogen tanks

2007

Dodge Zeo

powered by lithium-ion batteries
with a range of 400 km (250 miles)

Italdesign /Quaranta

inspired by the 1968
Bizzarrini Manta

2008

2025 Volkswagen Aquablues

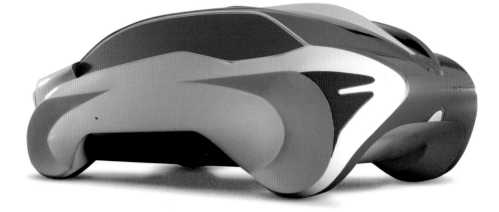

recreating
the spirit of the
VW minibus in an
amphibious car

Design by
Inn Whan Kim

2008

Lotus Extreme
Off-Roader

2008

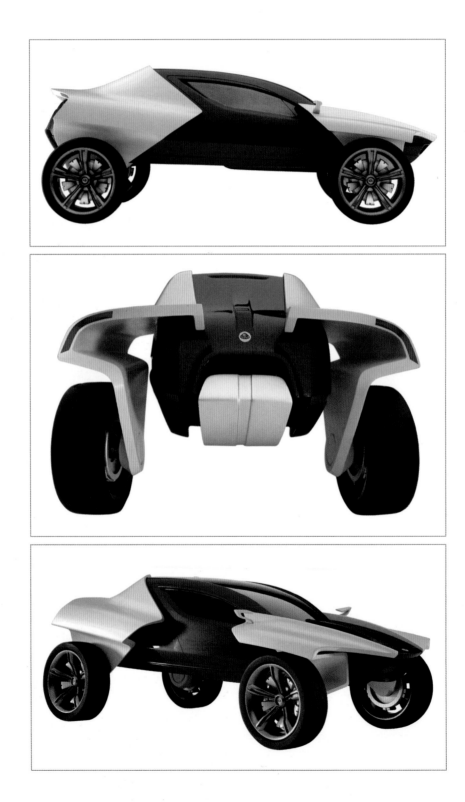

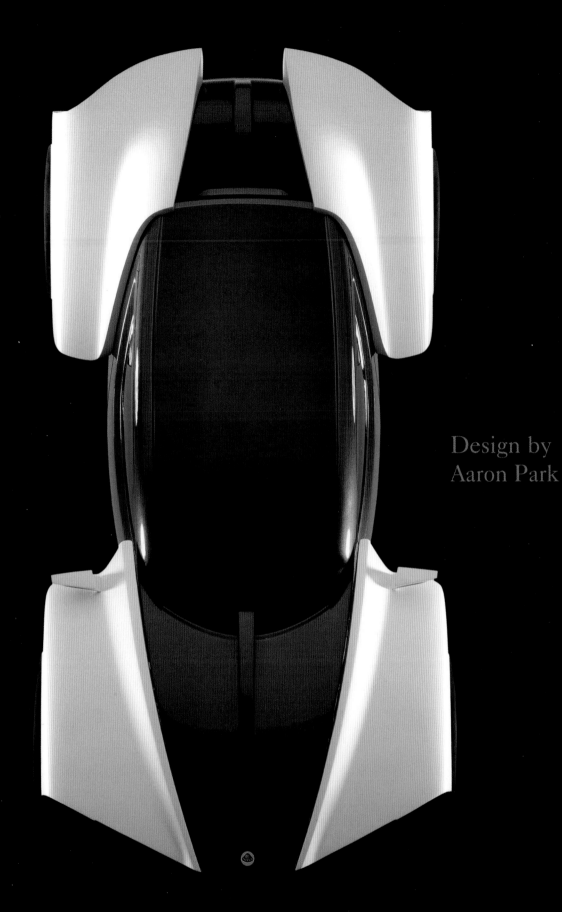

Design by
Aaron Park

a vehicle that can go over any
terrain condition imaginable

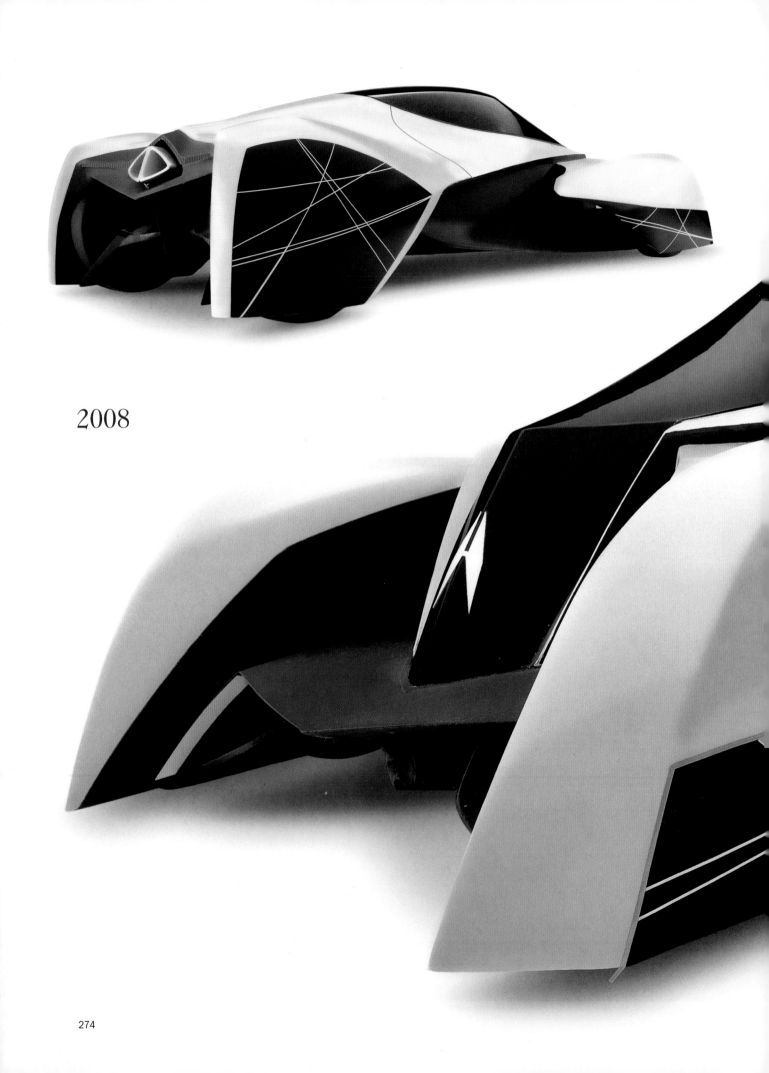

2008

Acura Living Machine Experiment (LMX)

seeks to integrate
the man/machine
experience in a living
breathing machine

Design by Calvin Luk

Audi eSpira / Audi eOra

eSpira, or Aspiration: created as an extension
of the human body and its senses

eOra, or Essence: this is a very dynamic
and efficient sports car

this prototype, unveiled in Shanghai in 2010,
stands as a futuristic solution to get around
the city traffic

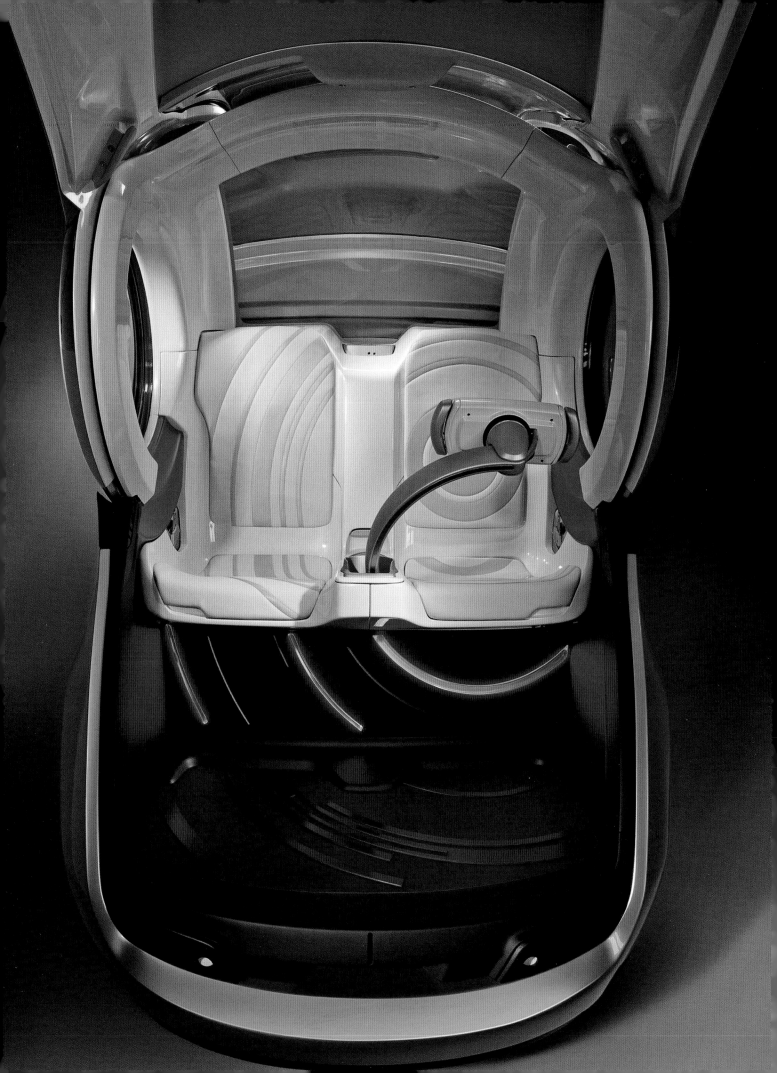

EN-V means
Electric Net
worked-Vehicle
and is the fruit
of the partnership
between
General Motors
and Shanghai
Automotive
Industry Corp.
Group

Cadillac / Aera

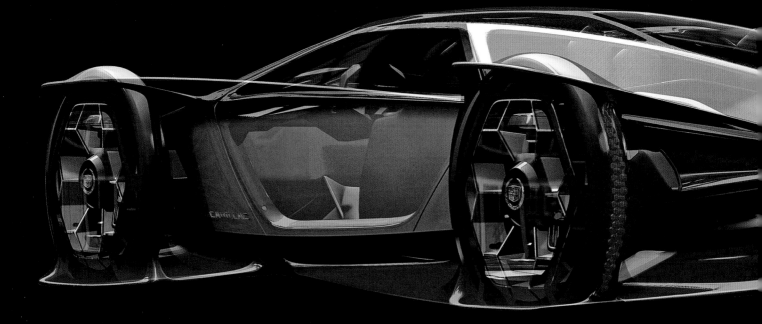

2010

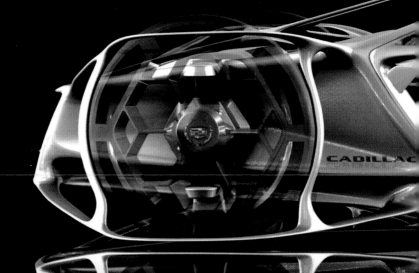

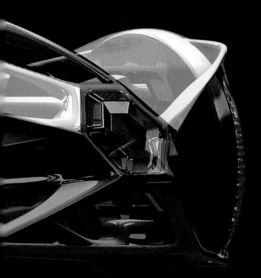

this model is the American House's answer to the new "Art Science" philosophy: weighing about 990 lb. (450 kg) and can run 930 mi. (1,500 km) on a full tank

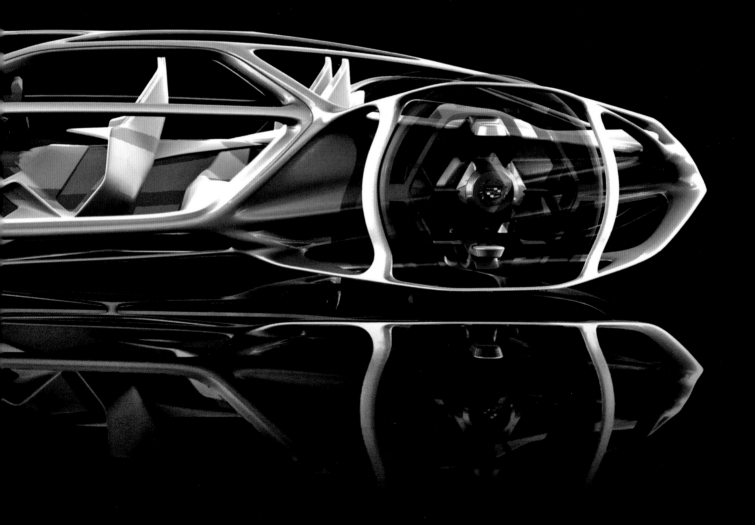

Index

Photo credits

Art Center College of Design: page 1

Bertone, Communication Direction: pages 69, 156-157

Buick Archives: pages 126-127

Car Culture/Corbis: pages 22-23, 24, 25, 252-253

Daimler Chrysler Media Archives: pages 92-93, 93, 130, 131

Citroën Communication: pages 242-243

Archivio Fioravanti s.r.l.: pages 96-97, 106-107, 264-265

Ford Motor Company: pages 142-143, 248-249

Michael Furman Photography: pages 10-11, 26-27, 81, 102-103

General Motors Media Archive: pages 118-119, 136-137, 148-149, 172-173, 174-175, 200, 201, 202-203, 204-205, 244, 245, 280, 281, 282, 283, 284-285

Henry Ford Museum: pages 53

Maggi & Maggi: pages 28-29

Mark Scheuern/Alamy: pages 266-267

Matra Archive: pages 116-117

Mazda Motor Corporation: pages 176, 177, 188, 189

Paolo Patrizi/Alamy: page 228

Peter Vann: pages 52-53

Pininfarina S.p.a.: pages 120, 124-125, 162-163, 150-151, 154-155

Ron Kimball Studios: pages 12, 30-31, 32-33, 34-35, 35, 36-37, 38, 39, 40-41, 46-47, 66-67, 68-69, 86-87, 88-89, 90-91, 98-99, 144-145, 152-153, 162-163, 164-165, 167, 168-169, 170-171, 180-181, 186-187, 190-191, 194-195, 232-233, 250-251, 254-255, 256-257, 258-259, 260-261

Toyama Tatsuyuki/Gamma/Contrasto: page 284

Toyota Motor Corporation: pages 234, 235, 236, 237

Transtock/Corbis: pages 44-45

Fotostudio Zumbrunn: pages 16-17, 26-27, 20-21, 21, 42, 43, 48-49, 50-51, 54, 58-59, 60-61, 62-63, 64-65, 65, 70-71, 72, 72-73, 78-79, 104, 104-105, 114-115, 132-133, 238-239

Courtesy of:

Art Center College of Design: pages 270-271, 272, 273, 274-275, 276-277

Audi Ag/Audi Media Services: pages 84-85, 158, 159, 192-193, 278-279

BMW AG: pages 210-211, 220, 220-221, 221

Fiat Group Automobiles: pages 206-207, 208-209

Ford Motor Company: pages 216 top and bottom, 216-217

Honda Auto: pages 218-219, 219

Italdesign Giugiaro S.p.a.: pages 74-75, 76-77, 94-95, 108-109, 110-111, 112-113, 134-135, 138-139, 146-147, 262, 263, 268, 269

Jaguar Cars Ltd: pages 202-203, 204-205

McLaren Automotive: pages 224-225, 225 top, 225 center

Nissan Motor Co. Ltd.: pages 212-213 top and bottom, 213

Peugeot Automobili Italia: pages 214 top and bottom, 215

Pininfarina S.p.a.: pages 226, 226-227, 227

Toyota Motor Corporation: pages 222, 223 top, center and bottom

Author

Jon Stroud is a writer, photographer specialising in sport and automotive subjects. He is a regular contributor to a wide range of publications in his native United Kingdom, Ireland and North America covering major sporting events including Formula 1 and the Superbike World Championship. When not in front of a computer or behind a camera he is usually to be found on a race circuit riding motorcycles very quickly.

Cover: Bmw Gina. © Courtesy of BMW Nord America, LLC

Back cover: Alé Fuel Vapor. © Kimball Stock

METRO BOOKS
New York

An Imprint of Sterling Publishing
387 Park Avenue South
New York, NY 10016

ISBN 978-1-4351-5006-5

For information about custom editions, special sales, and premium
and corporate purchases, please contact Sterling Special Sales at
800-805-5489 or specialsales@sterlingpublishing.com.

Manufactured in China

2 4 6 8 10 9 7 5 3 1

www.sterlingpublishing.com